Live Ar

edited by
Robert Ayers
and
David Butler

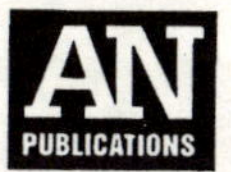

AN Publications

AN Publications exists to produce an information service for artists, craftspeople, photographers and those involved in art administration or education. It publishes the monthly magazine Artists Newsletter, Artists Handbooks, directories and Fact Packs. See pages 175 to 177 for details.

Acknowledgements

With thanks to Shirley Cameron, Simon Herbert, Bushy Kelly, Richard Layzell, Mike Stubbs and Jeni Walwin for help in shaping the book; and to Nicholas Sharp, solicitor, for consultancy on the copyright chapter.

Grant aid This book has been grant aided by the Arts Council

Editors Robert Ayers & David Butler

Sub-Editor Sharon McKee

Editorial assistance Tracey Musgrove

Index, Contacts & Further reading Caroline Lambert

Cover Design Edward Gainford Associates, Newcastle

Design & Layout Richard Padwick & Neil Southern

Printed Mayfair Printers, Print House, William Street, Sunderland, SR1 1UI

ISBN 0 907730 13 2

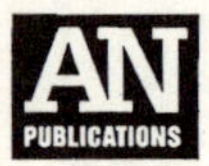

AN Publications is an imprint of
Artic Producers Publishing Co Ltd
PO Box 23, Sunderland SR4 6DG tel 091 567 3589

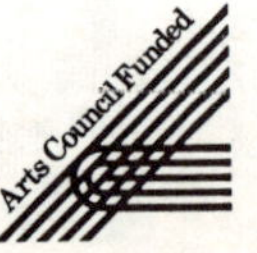

Contents

Profiles

The writers

Robert Ayers has been making performances for twenty years. He has been a tireless promoter of live art: as a writer, activist, and teacher. He is Head of Visual Arts at Nottingham Polytechnic.

Live art is when it's just you and the people. You can add in anything else you want, but if you forget this, you're rather missing the point.

Juliet Burgess is a solicitor. She no longer practises law. She curr exhibitions.

Live art presents an invitation to explore the human psyche. I find it provocative, disturbing, sensual, funny and vital.

David Butler is the commissioning editor of AN Publications and an artist working with live, time-based and participatory media.

Live art can't be kept by artist or audience. If it is good it becomes personal myth and can be revisited, if it's bad it can be forgotten.

Anne Cullis is administrator for a video production and training company in Birmingham, a freelance arts administrator and writer on visual arts, and editor of the National Artists Association 'Bulletin'.

Live art is people, places, processes, situations, objects, elements, time, movement, sound, light, smells, tastes, noises, touching, apprehension, excitement, uncertainty, materials, beauty, squalor.

Anna Douglas became interested in live art, because she was disenchanted with the tranquility of museum culture. Wishing to integrate people more into its artistic activity she programmed a performance series on the theme of Remembrance. She now works freelance in Liverpool initiating a range of projects.

Live art is an impossible term. It indicates activities which ask questions unbroachable in other art forms. But perhaps all I can be certain about is that it involves human interaction.

Bush Hartshorn is the artistic director of the Green Room, Manchester and Industrial and Domestic Theatre Contractors (established 1982). Acknowledgements to Steve Curtis, technical manager of the Green Room, for assistance in preparation of 'Legal Permissions'.

Live art is in the eye of the beholder.

Simon Herbert is the Performance and Visual Art Organiser at Projects UK, a Newcastle-based arts commissioning body. As an artist he has presented performances in Europe and Canada. He is a regular contributor to the arts press and catalogues.

Live Art in Britain is simply a promise. 90% of it is derivative, hollow, unsophisticated and prone to the tyrannies of dogma. Yet the other 10% fulfils the promise, subjecting the viewer to experiences impossible to get in any other art form.

Lois Keidan is currently Live Art Officer and New Collaborations Co-ordinator at the Arts Council. She has been Theatre Co-ordinator at the ICA and commission co-ordinator and publicist for performing arts at the Midland Group, Nottingham.

At the cutting edge of ideas and expression, live art is a rejection of single artform practice and a challenge to received ways of seeing, thinking and doing. Live art poses questions of not only what art is and can be, but where art is and what it is doing there.

Laurence Lane was a butcher for six years and then went to Crewe & Alsager College to study drama and sociology for three years. He is co-ordinator of the Quarter Club and has devised and performed on his own and with several other performance groups.

Live art is art that has an end and a beginning and while it exists has at least one living being as an integral part of it.

The writers

Richard Layzell has been regularly making live art since 1976. 'Bruno's Leg' was commissioned by the Tate Gallery in 1987 and 'Dancing on the Mountain' was shown across Canada and Britain in 1989. The 'House of Nation's' project, a large-scale installation and performance using waste materials, was shown in London and Nottingham in 1991. He teaches at Wimbledon School of Art, for the Open University, and at the Atsitsa Centre in Greece.

Live art is a lovely artform. Boundaries and audiences can be moved. Amazing risks are taken. Yet it remains hardly known and barely recognised. What a mistake.

Michael McMillan is a playwright for theatre and TV. He has worked as an arts administrator, programming several Black arts events, as a community publisher, editing a number of Black literary publications and in arts education. Recently he co-ordinated and directed a site specific installation with Keith Piper, 'Portrait of the Shopping Centre as a Cathedral'. He is currently writer for the Artists Agency residency working with people infected with HIV/AIDS in Newcastle. He will then be taking up a fellowship researching young people's theatre in the USA.

For I/myself, live art is art as a verb, action is implicit in its ephemeral exploitation of dynamic visual, physical/theatrical and spiritual/metaphysical forms. I seek to use it to reclaim a connection with an African approach to art that was created for and appreciated by the entire community, not just a priviliged, elite art consumer class.

Monica Ross works in time-based and installation media. She is a member of Red Herring Studios Brighton and is the BA Leader for the full-time section of the Critical Fine Art Practice Course at Central St Martins School of Art and Design.

Anne Seagrave began presenting performances whilst a student in the early '80s. She performed extensively in Britain, Europe and the USA until 1987. She attended the MA Fine Art in Belfast and has lived and worked in Dublin since 1989.

Live art is an idea, becoming a piece of work, presented by an artist, worth no more or less than any other artform, and commanding equal respect.

Françoise Sergy came from Switzerland to study at the London Contemporary Dance School. Further training in martial arts, New Dance, photography, and collaborations with women artists Gail Bourgeois, Honey Salvadori and Rosy Martin led to a series of live art works and photographic exhibitions toured nationally.

Live Art is... coming out, off the edge, poetry in motion, mute, gasping for breath... staring you in the face, kicking, dead, alive.

Mike Stubb's work encompasses film, video, mixed-media installations and performance and has been shown in Britain, Europe and Australia. He is the Artistic Co-ordinator of Hull Time Based Arts, a cooperative of artists working with music, film, performance, sculptural installation and video.

Live art is one that does not hang on walls easily and falls off plinths.

SuAndi is a performance poet and writer. Her voices and characters have entertained, shocked and emotionally stirred people of all ages. She is the cultural director voluntary of the Black Arts Alliance.

Live Art is musical, spontaneity, visual freedom of expression, improvisation, it's a theatre without a script. That's it. It's a theatre without a script.

Jennifer Walwin is currently the arts development consultant for the Broadgate Estates, London EC2. From 1978-83 she was exhibitions organiser at Southhill Park Arts Centre. From 1983-87 she was the combined arts officer and from 1987-90 the live art officer at the Arts Council of Great Britain.

Live art was originally used to describe performance work which had emerged from a fine art tradition. Artists were considered to be an integral part of this work which existed during a specific period of time and created no permanent object. More recently live art has come to embrace a range of experimental, multi-media form practices.

Mark Whitelaw is an artist who works with Eddie Aylward to form the Glee Club Performance Company.

About this book

'Live Art' was written by artists experienced in the making of live art, by its promoters and administrators, and by those with an understanding of, and particular sympathy for live art. It was written to inform, encourage and empower artists.

In preparation, we spent a good deal of time – and took a lot of advice – considering precisely what the book should include. Each contributor was asked to write about an aspect of live art in which we feel they are expert, and each was trusted to give that material their own interpretation. Given the wide range of activities that fall under the term 'live art', it was our conviction that maintaining the flavour of each of the contributions outweighed the need to give the book a seamless consistency.

We went further to reflect the breadth of live art's possibilities by compiling a questionaire and inviting many artists to relate their experiences. The response to this produced a wealth of information – far more than we could use. The questionnaires were numbered and the information was used for side notes throughout the book and for the full page examples with photographs. We looked for comments that counterpoint what the book is saying. We looked for a variety of live art practice. Only after we had chosen did we put names to the comments.

The first five chapters deal with the 'why' of live art. The remainder of the book looks at the 'how'. This is not a neat split. In all artforms theory and practice go hand in hand. But with live art the context and content of the work are paramount motivators in opening up new possibilities for artists and audience. The structure of thok reflects this.

We believe that, although it is no how-to-do-it guide, this book provides a coherent introduction to live art practices, from basic attitudes through seeking a formal training in live art to the most detailed questions of contracts and the law.

'Live Art' is a handbook has a utility for all sorts of readers: from the relatively inexperienced artist embarking upon their career with little or no knowledge of live art practice, to the artist who has been working in other forms and is turning to live art for the first time, to the experienced live artist who can consult this book for specific information or advice. Also we hope this potential readership might take in non-artists, particularly promoters and administrators. Although this handbook was written primarily for the benefit of artists, one of its recurrent themes is the relationship between live art's makers and its promoters. If it can encourage that relationship by helping artists and administrators better understand one another's expectations, then it will have fulfilled at least one of our ambitions for it.

If it seems ambitious to imagine a relevance for so wide a readership, then we must note as well our awareness that for virtually everyone who reads it there will be things we have omitted, or worse got wrong. Differences of opinion are inevitable among live artists and any book that did not reflect this would mislead its readers. On the other hand, as far as exhaustiveness is concerned, we have not even attempted it – that would imply a finite number of possibilities available to live artists, which misses the point entirely. We have borne in mind not only that the notion of a single correct way of making live art is an absurdity, but also the converse: that live art's continued value and relevance is mirrored by the extent to which other live artists continue to come up with surprising, disconcerting new possibilities.

1 • Changing people's lives

by Robert Ayers

This book has been written to change things. It has been written by artists, writers and administrators who have been encouraged by the changes that have taken place in British artists' circumstances in the last decade or so – changes that are seen by some as reflecting the shift from modernism to post-modernism – but who feel that as far as live art in particular is concerned there is a good deal of ground yet to be covered.

Until relatively recently, for example, it seemed perfectly acceptable for the people who were writing histories of modernist art to just about ignore those artists whose work found its meaning and its rationale in social or political engagement. As we approach the enormously politicised conclusion of the twentieth century however, there has occurred a huge increase in the number of British artists who want their art to achieve precisely this sort of engagement. Unless their art can change the lives of its audience in other words, then in the minds of an increasing number of intelligent British artists, it will be no more than decoration, no less than academicism.

For artists who think these things are important, live art has enormous power – a power that derives from its simplicity. Uniquely among the whole range of activities that are currently called art, live art allows a direct and unmediated contact between artist and audience. It requires no object – no painting, sculpture, print or photograph – it requires no equipment, venue or agent, no intermediary of any sort to act between the person who makes the art and the person it affects. Consequently, for artists who value the directness of their communication with their audience, and for whom it is important to safeguard that communication from mediation, interpretation or distortion, live art has enormous attractions. Unlike any of the art forms that involve the making of objects, and unlike virtually all of the 'performing' arts as well, live art allows

Painting, for example, is limited by the fact that the essence of the painting is in the doing of it. The hopes, visions, fears, conflicts and triumphs of the artist occur in private and the finished work will reveal far less than is trapped within the paint. The completion of a painting is like the death of a friend whose life had held such promise.
Les Seavor

the artist to enter into the everyday lives of its audience and – quite literally – to touch them. And it is that moment free of preconceptions when flesh touches flesh, which as often as not is as unsettling – let's face it, as terrifying – for the artist as for the audience that, no matter what else they build upon it, is the essence of live art for many of the artists who make it.

This is not, of course, the whole story (and if it were, there would be no need for this book). In the first place, what many artists build upon that essence and into their live work is considerable. In any case it seems inevitable that the very special contact with its audience that live art can enjoy – that poignant, highly-charged, never-to-be-experienced-again moment of direct contact – means it is often beset by practical and administrative difficulties.

There are at least two reasons for this: it is still the case this late into its history that live art lacks (though many of us would wonder about the word 'lack') the set of conventions and easy expectations which was basic to the development of the critical, administrative and commercial support corps which has existed for well over a century for the makers of objects, and upon which they rely so heavily. Also the simple truth is that at each presentation – whatever that implies for the individual work – live art has, as it were, to be made anew. Whether it involves just the recollection by a single performer of a few simple movements, or the co-ordination of enormous resources of equipment and personnel, it can, at each presentation, go wrong. It does not matter how many times the work has been presented, the artists and those who support and collaborate with them, each time face the problems of making the thing actual, of making it work, whereas the object-maker sorted it out once and for all in their studio, probably months before the art ever made contact with its audience.

There are then, despite live art's apparent simplicity, many easier, cheaper and less stressful ways of making art. It is clearly an activity that appeals to a certain sort of artistic personality: one not only drawn to its advantages, but willing as well to put enormous energies into overcoming its disadvantages. Almost every maker of live art has had the experience of having to act as their own administrator, promoter or agent; has known and accepted having to create the circumstances in which their art can be presented in the first place. That has certainly been the experience of those of us who have contributed to this book, and our experience is that live art is not immune to mediation. In fact, somewhat ironically,

It is this element of risk, whereby the performer/artist(s) is left open to the collective intervention of the viewer or the unforeseen event that I am interested in.
Tim Brennan

its vulnerability in the moment of its re-creation in the presence of its audience makes it that much more susceptible to distortion. We have all had the dispiriting experience of seeing how easily our live work can be knocked little by little out of shape by considerations we might have thought external to it: compliance with health and safety regulations, for example, or the house rules of the institution in which it is being presented, or the whims of the administrator, or the timing of the technicians' tea-break, or something as simple and stupid as the size, shape or colour of a room. And that was why we felt a handbook of this sort was necessary: not only as a source of information that might allow artists to anticipate as many of those 'external considerations' as possible but also to encourage an attitude to not see them as external in the first place. An attitude to see any consideration that might affect the presentation of an artist's work as falling within the artist's proper domain, and which might allow artists to better control, to eventually take control of the circumstances in which their art is made and presented. What this attitude assumes, of course, and what we have assumed in our readers, is a well-developed sense of responsibility – one that might almost be thought of as a sort of pride – in their work, and in its presentation.

This is an artist for whom the social power of their work involves obligations as well as opportunities. Certainly not the sort of artist who sees themselves as an aesthetic or social guerilla, making art on a hit-and-run (and hit-or-miss) basis, and relishing the shock waves they leave in their wake. Of course – as many of us now realise – imagining that an artist might function in this way relies upon precisely those modernist mythologies this book has been written to overturn but which, it is distressing to note, are still being propagated by the ageing staff of art schools up and down the country. It is exactly this modernist irresponsibility – *'My responsibilities end when I put the paint brush down',* is how I recall one artist expressing it – that means it was necessary to produce a book of this sort. We have to win back the control of the structures that condition the making and showing of our art precisely because the people who were in our shoes fifteen and twenty years ago found in this sort of attitude such a cosy refuge from those responsibilities – they tended to dismiss them as 'administration' – that we feel are a basic part of the artist's activity.

If that means that there is in the attitude of our predecessors a contempt for other artists, then another aspect of modernist thinking that this book has been written to overturn is what amounts to a contempt for art's audience. It is ironic that, under modernism, the enormous social potential of live art was often forgotten in favour of a perverse and private purism. It became the preserve of an in-crowd of initiates, concerned itself only with them, and suffered as a consequence a barren introspection in the work itself, and the contempt of more and more of exactly those people who might have made up its audience. This book sees a concern with audience as being basic to live art's power. If art is going to change the lives of its audience it is only sensible to give some thought as to who that audience might be. It registers that an audience might take many different forms and it encourages the recurrent asking of the question, 'Who is this art for?' and a realisation that to allow the answer to this to affect the shape of the work is no abandonment of the work's integrity but rather an acknowledgement of its flexibility, its strength and its potential.

Attitude to audience evolves and changes like every other aspect of a creative practice.... On many levels I think of it as a privilege that they are there. So, I don't want to abuse this privilege, it's only too easy to wind an audience up, to intimidate them, to frighten them. The performer is in a very powerful position.
Richard Layzell

So, in considering why this book has been written, we need to register both short-term and long-term reasons, and a somewhat ironic relationship between the two. In the first instance, we have set ourselves the task of describing, as usefully as we might, the current state of affairs, the world in which performance artists find themselves working presently. But this is a world which many of us regard as basically flawed in that it is one in which artists too often have to respond to the initiatives of others and, worse, have to contend with their decisions. It is precisely that world which we want to change fundamentally. To this extent, this book will only have succeeded when we do not need it any more.

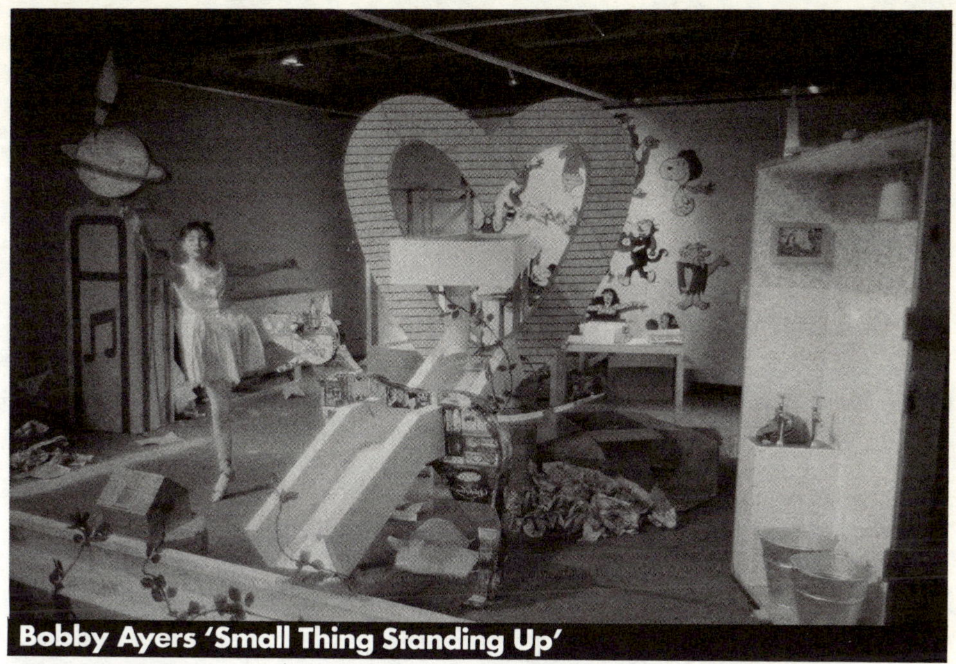

Bobby Ayers 'Small Thing Standing Up'

Having made site-specific, one-off performances with ad hoc companies for a number of years, and having during that time grown accustomed to comments like, 'Your problem is, you do all of your performances in secret' (although I certainly didn't) 'Small Thing Standing Up' was made with the specific intention that it should be easily transportable, make relatively few demands of its venue, and thus be infinitely repeatable. My original idea had been to make a performance to fit in a suitcase. Eventually it was a tight squeeze for the back of a Transit. I performed it seventeen times in venues ranging from art galleries and museums to colleges, pubs, a night club, and a gymnasium. I think it was probably seen by more people than all of my other performances put together although I am aware that the intensity of experience that the audience took away from it was rather slighter than from some of the other pieces. For some reason or another I had saddled myself with the notion that 'Small Thing Standing Up' should be identical on every restaging. Not surprisingly, after a couple of years I got rather tired of it. I allowed it to mutate into 'Another Small Thing Standing Up' and, with the reverse assumption that it will never be the same twice, still very occasionally perform it.

2 • Critical action

by Monica Ross

'Art is not magic, it is not mumbo jumbo, it is not a mere thing and it is also not nothing'.
Martha Rosler,
'Issues' catalogue,
ICA, 1980

The paradox of high modernist notions of art practice occurring in an autonomous realm away from the broader social sphere was that, while this elevated some artists (the few) to special individual status, it also, effectively, marginalised and dislocated artists (the many) from a more central role in society. This 'autonomous realm' might be characterised as only the studio, the gallery and the art market economy.

One extreme effect of this dislocation has been a caricatured perception of the artist as an isolated individual whose gestures originate from within a perpetual state of social alienation – a perception which has often been deeply internalised by artists themselves and supported by the art school system.

This is not to deny that powerful art work can originate from an opposition to given values and structures in society. But social alienation is not an exclusive characteristic of the artist. So, how can such work become more than a neatly contained howling in the wind, connect with the social alienation of others, maintain meaning and a cutting edge in the face of either dismissive stereotyping or relegation to the obscure margins (rarefied or not) of cultural experience?

Public art

'Do you think performance art has anything to offer within the public art arena?' was a question asked at a conference on public art and education in 1988.

The irony of this question lies in the fact that the entire history and practice of live art, rather than being marginal to the public art debate actually provides examples of art practice for that debate. This history has been one of direct interaction with one kind of audience or another; direct intervention into one public space or another; an engagement with specific audiences or sites often lying at the heart of the work. Since the 1970s, performance artists have been instrumental in initiating the debates and practices that have opened up the possibilities and provided models for making and presenting art in broader social arenas than those of the half-empty galleries of that period. Among others, Hull Time-Based Arts group is an impressive example in Britain. A major performance work such as 'In Mourning and In Rage' by the American artist Suzanne Lacey is another. This broke new ground in its dramatic articulation of a specific community crisis, locally on the streets and at national and international levels in major galleries and through a skilful use of communications and documentation media (TV networks, radio and press).

'In Mourning and In Rage', 1979-1980, The Drama Review, issue on Suzanne Lacey's work. MIT Press, New York, Spring 1988

Despite this, the above question can still be asked. Live art does have a paradoxical position within public art. It provides an example for public art practice which is undermined by its historical association with avant-gardism, with caricatures of the artist as being socially estranged, as cultural guerrilla, as bizarre, as unreliable. This contributes to the marginalisation of live art within a 'public art' debate which is fraught with conflicting attitudes and is already looking stifled and over-determined by the rise of an over-bureaucratised and basically conservative public art establishment.

The legacy of avant-gardism calls up fixed fears of the unsafe and unpredictable in live art from the establishment, its uncertain clients and its wary sponsors. 'But will it last?' is apparently a frequent question posed by clients of Public Art Commissioning Agency.

Vivien Lovell, Director Public Art Commissioning Agency at Public Art & Artists Conference, Birmingham, 1990

Live artists themselves have often maintained an allegiance to the avant-garde characterisation of the artist: partly from a commitment to staying beyond the deadening hands of institutionalisation and categorisation, but also because of the mythic status of avant-gardism as the rebellious catalyst essential to the continued progress of modernism. This may be a suitable, and even a successful position, for some artists who define their arena within the exclusion zone of the art market place, but live artists who want to make work within a broader social arena need to re-examine their own relation to both this myth, and the other historical and contemporary practices in live art which have a powerful role to play within the broader public arena. If not, live art in all its forms will continue to be marginalised and art as fixture (the monument), the absolute antithesis of time-based work, fixed meanings rather than dialectics will continue to monopolise, largely unchallenged, the plaza, the garden festival or any other available roundabout.

Moving out/Moving in

In moving towards making work beyond any currently available art circuits (just as within them) it is important to be familiar with the relevant debates and practices which make up the discourse that your own work will participate in and be defined by. As I've attempted to describe above, such histories and debates, together with others, mediate the artist's work, in production and reception, wherever it happens to occur; fairs, festivals, warehouses or galleries. (Since when were the latter not public places?) Your practical knowledge and appropriate social and technical skills obviously need to be adequate to any given situation (as in never go anywhere without your own tool box). Equally you need to be able to find funding for your work. This handbook offers a wealth of such advice, but, even armed with it, most skills are still more likely to be gained from experience, productive failures, trial and error. There are no formulas for making successful or even competent work in non-gallery situations. Nor should there be. Attitudes, however, abound. In fact, as many possibilities for work exist as do diverse artists and audiences. It is the realisation of these diversities that is crucial to the maintenance of dynamic, unfixed art practices in the social domain. Central to achieving this, I would suggest, is the development by artists of theories of practice which can interrogate the prevailing winds of attitude (art and social) instead of being buffeted about or led by them.

Within any particular artist's practice, such theories need to be sensitive enough to be revised on encounter with new knowledge, events and influences, but also to have enough strength and integrity to guide decision-making processes, particularly those affecting matters of refusal, compromise, context and choice.

What I am suggesting is a strategy of empowerment together with information gathering. It is this process, rather than making definitive recommendations (there are already too many) as to what a 'public' or 'social' practice should be, that I want to discuss. I would suggest, for instance, the following are some key questions and terms which any artist embarking on 'public' or 'social' practices, who wants to create work of integrity, should seriously consider.

Theories & critiques

Where do you place your art practice and approach on a scale between such currently polarised positions as: good art has universal meaning and will stand up for itself anywhere regardless of its site or audience;

and it's opposition: meaningful art is produced out of an interactive and knowledgeable relationship with its audience or host communities.

The first position largely originates from a modernist standpoint. It assumes art has essential meanings which transcend the social and defines the artist's position as autonomous or incidental to the social, rather than as an integratedly active agent.

It denies that the play of social and cultural difference affects the construction of meaning, or that the spectator has an active role in such; or that the physical, social and historical aspects of the context or site will be as significant to the making of art as its formal characteristics. Extended criticism includes arguments suggesting cultural condescension or imperialism; the domination of artistic values, taste and meaning, of one social group by another. This position is also likely to prioritise the artist's practice as painter, sculptor, performer.

The second position originates from post-modern critiques, including those of film and feminist theory. Firstly, it places the artist as a socially aware, and socially produced, individual who will probably use research and consultative strategies in choosing a process which includes the audience and context in the developing new work. This also suggests the artist's strength lies in adaptable attitudes; a capacity to acquire new skills as needed. The artist is credited as being an imaginative, intellectual and technically agile individual who is responsive to situations in form, subject and media, rather than always having pre-determined them (or being determined by them). Such an artistic base is historically closer to conceptual art and live art than practices defined by a single medium.

Who are you making work for?

One definition of community by Raymond Williams in 'Key Words' is *'Community: A network of social relationships and a sharing of common meanings. Since our way of seeing things is our way of living the process of communication is the process of community. In this sense a community can be world, a continent, a country, a region, a town, a village or a few houses near a pub.'*

Do you experience yourself as, amongst other things, being an 'anybody', an 'ordinary person'; that is a member of a public which shares common meanings? Or do you think of yourself as being separate from the public? Is your understanding of the public one of a large anonymous mass or is it of specific groups, ones that might be immediately available and local to you; a street, workmates, friends, family? Or groups (of ideas, issues and theories as well as apparent social and cultural formations) nationally or internationally with whom you identify, share concerns, want to contest, unravel, represent, be in debate with? That is, what are the possible communities of your work?

Audiences & their interaction

Post-modernist theories have unpacked generalisations of the public into richly differentiated subjects and groups whose experiences of an artwork will differ according to race, gender, class, health, age, culture and history. Such complex publics are then acknowledged to be active readers, viewers and consumers of art rather than passive recipients of a gift bestowed.

This standpoint collapses boundaries between artist, art and audience, since a line resists being drawn as to who is actually producing the meaning of the work – an area long fascinating and important in live art. Such re-assessments of viewing or consuming art also re-charge established performance positions that the value of the work resides, not in its permanence or increase in market value, but in its specific occurrence and the residual effect. This argument re-asserts the difference between the economy of live work (on the levels of both meaning and money) and that of a high modernist practice determined by the economy of the art market. From this position also the fact that some live works will only occur once, and with specific audiences, continues to bear credit for live art, both as a social art practice and as an alternative to the 'monument' tendency of much public art thinking.

Counter arguments

Common criticisms levelled at social art practices are that: such art will be detrimentally over-identified with its audience (can it tour?); formal considerations will be forfeit to the pre-eminence of subject matter (politics?); the work will be over-determined by its social concerns (will it last?); the artist's freedom will be effectively diminished by art being accomplished through 'art by committee' processes.

Such work is then criticised as having been reduced to the level of a service, craft skill, illustration, propaganda or entertainment. In a word, to being parochial and therefore mediocre and amateur – bad art or not art at all. Such work is then often dismissed as marginal – but to what, to whom?

Do not decoration, craft skill and entertainment also play a major role in the quality of our lives? Pleasure, comfort, fantasy? On the other hand, one cannot argue that all social practice does not produce parochial work, because some of it undoubtedly does. Much 'public art', whatever its critical origin, is not only lamentably lacking in artistic ambition but is even banal. But such criticism also raises questions of value; whose values, which values?

The validity of any critical position, just like an art practice, is also open to questioning. The artist needs to establish which critical criteria are relevant to their own practice. Where, for instance, was a particular work made? For whom? Most significantly, why? How was it received? Who considers the work to be parochial and does their view outweigh the value of its audience's reaction, which may have been appreciative? To which parts of the work are such criticisms being aimed? Does artistic integrity only reside in the final product and not also in its processes of production? The parallel with live art is very clear here. Context-specific art making processes are unlikely to be directly transferable or marketable in the conventional art-world sense. The only person likely to earn money from them is probably the artist. The values of socially specific practices then, would seem to demand broader critical frameworks than those rooted only in gallery practice. This indicates the need for broader debates than one polarised between parochialism and universalism, and asks for a greater interest, by both artists and administrators, in extending their own critical awareness.

Art journals and their critics, until recently sparse contributors to this debate, could provide a more fruitful platform. Despite the fact work in the public or social domain frequently enjoys larger audiences than its gallery counterpart, critically it is still treated as being marginal to gallery work as the main artistic issue. So who is being parochial here? On the other hand if 'public art' was being produced and addressed within as serious a critical framework as some gallery art, would mediocrity in 'public art' be an issue of such concern at all?

Parochial? Marginal? Central?

Are the concerns of the residents in an old people's home necessarily parochial? Is such a context together with those of leisure centres, community events and fairs, the DHSS, international banking systems

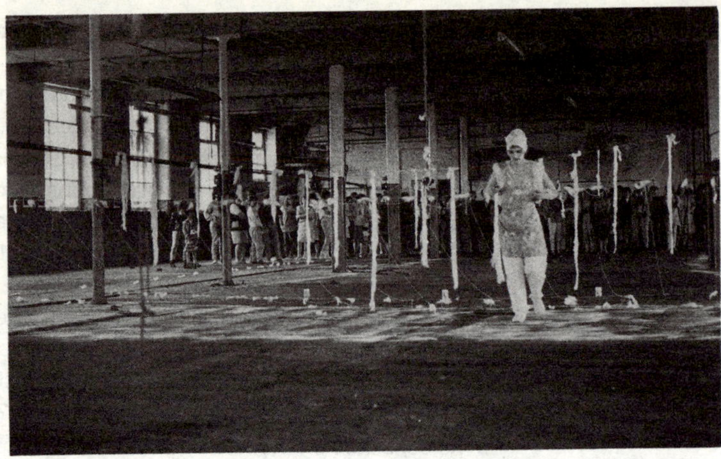

A Ghost in the Spinning Mill, Monica Ross, **1985. Lunchtime performance for employees of Besco Ltd, Barchant Mill, Rochdale.** ***Photo:*** *Patsy Mullan*

marginal to the art world or is it the reverse? (Consider the role of business sponsorship). Are terms like 'marginal' or 'central' any longer relevant in a system of economic and political linkage between one social institution and another? Why should art-making in a Dundee hospital have become more suggestive of decoration than major art? May not such an artist and their public also be subject to racism, sexism and ageism, susceptible to sexual desire, fantasy and pleasure; to the Aids virus or the Greenhouse effect? Aren't they also watching 'Neighbours', 'The News at Ten', foreign movies, drinking coffee and Coca-Cola with their curry or pizza?

Is not parochial art then, an art which, together with ignoring contemporary cultural debate, also ignores that we are all participants and consumers in a global culture to some extent, whatever the specifics of our age, race, gender, or the place where we work and live?

If so, does such an art not risk being just as guilty of 'cultural condescension' as that of its critical opposition?

Who is taking the initiative?

One value of the tension between 'social' and 'universal' based practices is that it at least keeps the artist's role, particularly the artist's integrity, on the agenda. It is a tension which, at extreme moments, can manifest concerns common to both camps. A term such as 'parachute art' criticises making and placing art with no concern for its social context whereas a term such as 'parachutism' promotes art as a radical practice

Term, or tactic, raised in discussions at the Art, Culture & Society Conference, Oxford Museum of Modern Art, 1990

of autonomous shock tactics. 'Parachute art' is a term of abuse linked to that of 'turds in the plaza'. 'Parachutism', artist as cultural guerrilla, signals a nostalgic tendency to revive the shade of avant-gardism. Both terms raise questions of power.

Live art is often an art of urgency and immediacy. Many artists feel just as dis-empowered by, and distanced from, the bureaucratic commissioning and funding structures of large sectors of the public art arena (the developers asking will it last?) as they do by the limitations of gallery work. Have these structures eroded the creative initiative (power) of artists in an arena largely initiated by them in the first place? Don't cries of 'parachuting' from either camp merely signal such a situation?

Towards an integrity of practice

Who determines an artist's role in any situation (decorator, entertainer or initiator)? Are the factors operating restrictive, or creative and challenging? What about the time-frame? (Can you fill this space? Do you want to be scheduled between the fire-eaters and the raffle? Do you want to wait six months?) Are these questions pre-determined or collaboratively resolved between the artist, the audience, the commissioners, the organisers and the sponsors? Is the artist included in all such discussions from the outset? If not, when?

Do you see your artistic identity as being singly defined or do you have the capacity to inhabit different categories: sensor, negotiator, conscience, researcher, catalyst, enabler, provocateur, fund-raiser, mediator or curator? There are many possibilities. Do you think your work can change things? Even for a moment – from the subtlest effects of life enhancement and experiences of pleasure to being 'part of a broad social movement for change?' What are your strengths; artistic, social; experiences and knowledges? Or your obsessions? Do these affect your art practice and choice of contexts? Do you need, or are you flexible enough, to take on new skills and approaches as necessary? Do you make independent choices of context for your work or are you mainly interested in opportunities that are pre-briefed by a commissioner or sponsor? How much work would you want to make over a given period of time? Does waiting on the competitive possibilities of one or two commissions a year provide an adequate framework for your work to develop? Do the two oppositions of artist as cultural guerrilla and artist as inclusive social agent have to be exclusively distinct? Are there not other possibilities which might combine and develop the strengths of both practices?

In conclusion

Many artists work across the gallery/public domain divide to the enrichment of both contexts. However, only a comparatively few art agencies exist in this country which have a commitment to instigating and supporting live art within public spaces and social contexts. Social art practices return the initiative to artists to generate and expand this meagre framework to one of greater opportunity both for making their work, defining their own terms, and engaging with the reception of that work. Working in the public or social sector no more obliges the artist to only give people what they appear to want than it does them to acquire street-theatre skills. The making of 'good art', art of integrity and meaning, always involves the artist in risk-taking. There are few contexts more risky, uncertain, difficult and challenging than those beyond the given art circuit: the terminally ill children's ward, the picket line, the myriad of a county fair. The inhabitants of these are likely to be more vocal and active commentators than the well-trained gallery goer. The support systems, the art press and the technical help are also not likely to be there (bring your own).

It can be hard work, take a great deal of sensitivity to other people's work loads and commitments, to unravel and work within the bureaucratic organisation and internal politics of even an apparently straight forward social context. On the other hand, the benefits to an artist working as an 'anybody' or inclusive member of a social group or within a set of shared ideas can be enormous. Choosing your own contexts dispenses with distant selectors, the sense of having to be approved of in order to make work (empowerment). The terrain that opens out is exactly what most artists need. Supportive, challenging, and appropriate contexts for their work; publics that are actually interested and engaged with both the process and the final product. Such interactions can stimulate the invention of different visual and physical languages, extending both the artist's and the community's experience of art, themselves and their potential. The host community may gain an art that it may not have known it wanted or had ever had the opportunity to imagine, but which it can utilise on many different levels: empowered to enjoy, criticise, debate, even become the guardian of.

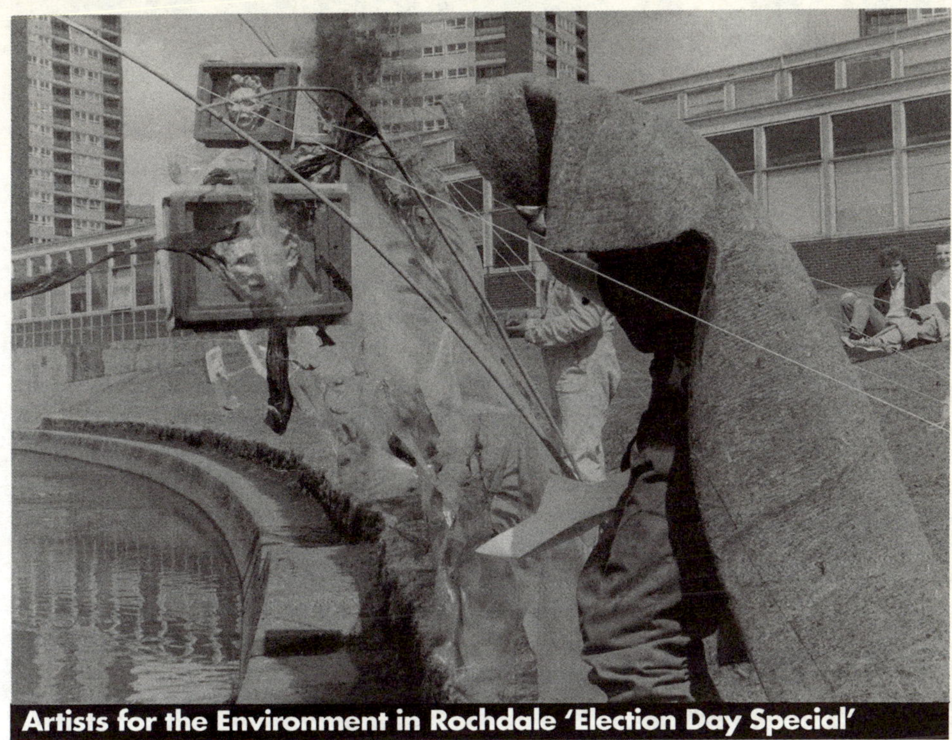

Artists for the Environment in Rochdale 'Election Day Special'

Live art patronage can be best evaluated in terms of how Europe perceives it. That British artists do considerably better on the continent relates directly to attitudes of the audience, and sectors of life by which they are composed. In the UK, where any art practice is scorned by the potential audience and therefore expected as a voluntary service, it is often the case that the state of cultural impoverishment limits the variation of communicative means. The consequent result for live artists of being expected to perform through subsidy and social responsibility means that their socialist values become honed to deal with moral dilemmas and inefficiency derived from the commissioner. This in turn prohibits the socialisation process of artists and their practice.

Artist initiatives are high on AFTER's policy agenda. So far, most projects have been workable. Whilst discovering new areas of finance for this activity, the bureaucracy machine quickly finds means to appropriate the funding base. It is perhaps just as well that artists' initiatives far outstrip the supply.

The photograph shows a voluntary street performance called 'Election Day Special' which coincided with the re-election of Margaret Thatcher as Prime Minister in 1988. Police stopped the performance outside Rochdale Town Hall. It was transferred to the banks of the River Roch and renamed 'Sold down the River and the Pedigree shows'.

3 • Personal histories

It seems to be a fact of life that every live artist has to rediscover for themselves the history of the activity. This fact is at once the source of live art's constant refreshment of itself and – particularly for audiences who have been around for a few years – one of its recurrent frustrations.

Just as almost every live artist will imagine different boundaries to their activity and, if pushed, will probably come up with their own characteristic definition of what live art is, it's as though each artist has to create their own history out of those precedents that are important to them. The frustration stems in some measure from the fact that even the most eloquent documentation of live art is rarely more than a pale shadow of the experience of the actual work. Because it is impossible for any of us to repeat the experience of the famous performance works of the past, those same infamous photographs are repeatedly reproduced – Yves Klein 'leaping' into the void, for example, or Joseph Beuys comforting that dead hare, or Jim Dine sprayed silver in a plastic mac – and seem to exercise a fascination for generation after generation of young artists who are drawn to live work. Paradoxically, it is equally true that once those Klein and Beuys and Dine photographs and descriptions have been pored over, thought about, re-enacted, and exorcised, each live artist is free to relate to their own personal history and, most excitingly, to build upon it the unique character of their own work.

Although this book is not the place for art history, it is probably worth noting most accounts of live art would tend to trace its roots to just about the time when photographic technology could capture, relatively casually, moving figures in ill-lit locations, which is to say, to the performances of the Italian futurists and the Cabaret Voltaire of the Zurich Dadas. The public and private behaviour of the surrealists tends to come next, and then the 'Action Painting' of Pollock and the other American artists who were most influenced by them. The charismatic John Cage is introduced to most histories at this point, and then those artists who occupied the related spheres of his influence: on the one hand Kaprow and the other makers of happenings, on the other Macunias, Higgins and the other artists who worked under the banner of Fluxus.

This, of course, is only one imperfect way of recounting the history. The remainder of this chapter is devoted to three individuals relating their own histories, their own versions of what matters to them. They reflect the need for artists, critics and the public to stretch definitions of 'art' – by repositioning it outside the gallery, in direct confrontation with audience; by recognising the way 'mainstream' definitions can exclude Black arts practices; by crossing artforms to introduce new modes of personal, social and political expression.

Beginnings in Britain

by Richard Layzell

'There was a score of sorts, arrived at by chance methods, but the performers also had a considerable freedom of action during the 45 minute performance. Their actions took place simultaneously, and included Cage reading one of his lectures from the upper rungs of a stepladder; Merce Cunningham dancing both around and amid the audience... Mary Caroline Richards and Charles Olsen reading their poems... Robert Rauschenberg playing scratchy records... two other people projecting movies and still pictures on the walls....This curious spectacle was wthout question the prototype of a whole series of improvisational events, called 'Happenings'.'
'Ahead of the Game' by Calvin Tomkins, Penguin, 1968.

By 1962 happenings were regularly shown in New York. The idea of a free-flowing art event in real time still conjures up the atmosphere of many live art performances, today. Britain in the 1960s saw similar experiments. The internationally recognised Destruction in Art Symposium, set up by John Latham and Gustav Metzger, took place in London in 1966 and stemmed from self-destructive art and ideas. The term 'event' was used rather than 'happening' and organisations like Eventstructure Research Group, WHSSHT, Artists Placement Group (APG), SPACE, AIR and Artists for Democracy began to evolve. The American artist Carolee Schneeman brought her happenings regularly to London and another American, Carlyle Reedy, took up residence:

'I came to London in 1964.... I was invited to work with WHSSHT, to create shows with John Latham, Stuart Brisley and others. We worked at Middle Earth. The first occasion, loud music drowned out my work with Peter Dockley... so, for the next show I acquired a piano-shaped stage with a place to lie, a place to sit, a place to stand.... I was on that stage in a semi-transparent dress for four hours, doing absolutely nothing at all of any interest, to see if I could be there in such a way as to become interesting... people were receptive to new ideas.... A period of heady experimentation gets coloured up by the media as though it were all mindless pop and drugs – here were

From an interview with Carlyle Reedy in 'Artists Newsletter', May 1988

real people, thinkers, awake, attacking social issues, relating perceptions to changing form… confrontations, as I would make with conventional theatre, Carolee Schneeman's Happenings, Events, art-life collectives of David Medalla….'

An exhibition at the ICA in London in 1969 'When Attitudes Become Form' brought together conceptual art and early performance art ideas from people like Joseph Beuys, Bruce McLean, Victor Burgin and Mario Merz. In the same year, the new wave of German artists, again including Beuys, were brought to the Edinburgh Festival by Richard Demarco under the title of 'Strategy Get Arts'. Out of this flurry of activity and influence, Stuart Brisley, Bruce McLean and Gilbert & George emerged as the closest to household names in early performance work. Stuart Brisley, in particular, gained considerable press coverage in Britain for his strenuous, punishing, durational 'events', sometimes involving self-imposed vomiting and soaking in baths of offal, etc. There was a parallel here to Hermann Nitsch and the Viennese Activists, with their ritual ripping open of animal carcasses and even near suicide. Bruce McLean's 'Nice Style Pose Band' was more clean-cut, as were Gilbert & George with 'Underneath the Arches':

From an interview with Gilbert & George in 'Performance Magazine' No 29, 1984

'It was just so new, happening in the middle of the Fluxus movement, which we disliked. We disliked the form, everyone rolling on the floor, dirty. We wanted to make a bronze sculpture come alive… a sculpture for everybody that everybody could understand, not where they thought 'What the devil's happening?'

Performance groups emerged all over the country, including Shirley Cameron and Roland Miller, Welfare State, The People Show and Forkbeard Fantasy, all of which are still active today.

The broader context for much of this 'live' work was a profound dissatisfaction with the commercial gallery system. Painting and sculpture were in decline. Conceptual art, live events and artists' films offered an alternative, one which appeared to be non-commercial and therefore a challenge to the gallery system, where art was equated with commodity. Subsequent history has shown that conceptual art and installations can indeed be absorbed by the art market, notably with the late Joseph Beuys and many of the American conceptualists, but live art still maintains its ground as a form which cannot be bought.

The second generation

In the 1970s and early 80s, 'performance art' became the recognised label, internationally, for what became seen both as a movement and an established art form. Once the sparks had settled and many extreme, hard-to-repeat actions and gestures had been made, clearing the ground, the way forward began to suggest itself. Perhaps there were more subtle ways of making an impact on an audience. Perhaps the traditions of theatre and dance didn't have to be rejected out of hand.

In Britain, several significant women artists began working in this expanding field, one which offered a possibly less male-dominated future, given its brief history. Rose English, Sally Potter, Annabel Nicholson, Tina Keane, Rose Finn-Kelcey, Anne Bean and Rose Garrard were regularly performing and producing related works. Fran Hegarty's teaching at Sheffield Polytechnic provided inspiration for many, as did Alastair MacLennan's in Belfast. In London, a lot of activity centred around the Acme Gallery and the AIR Gallery and later at the Diorama. Regional museums and art centres were increasingly mounting festivals or seasons of performance. A series of International Performance Festivals in Lyon, France, were echoed by the Bracknell Performance Festival in England. The National Review of Live Art began.

I was working at the Acme Gallery in the late 1970s and I've retained some lasting memories and images of the time:

- Marc Chaimowicz and co-performer 'fade'-ing behind screens, to the accompaniment of Mahler;
- Steve Cripps creating an explosion which resulted in an asphyxiated audience leaving within seconds and the fire brigade arriving seconds later;
- Annabel Nicholson leading her audience by lantern and speaking about fireflies with a quiet intensity;
- Bruce Lacy and Jill Bruce, coated in a thin film of mud and feathers, running up the rough wooden structure which led them through the roof of the gallery towards closer contact with the stars;
- Kerry Trengrove being sealed inside a breeze-block cell, then digging his way out for eight days, while the international media looked on;
- Hannah O'Shea intoning her 'Litany of Women Artists';
- Marty St James dressed as a radish.

This was a richly expansive period, which saw performance art begin to extend beyond the sphere of fine art. In the 1980s this process continued and there was a clear cross-fertilisation between art forms, in the way that Dada's 'Cabaret Voltaire' (made up artists, poets, musicians and writers) had indicated, back in 1916. Performers from experimental dance and theatre began to collaborate with artists or to draw ideas from the live art arena. The line between a performance group (like Dogs in Honey) and a theatre group (like Forced Entertainment, also Sheffield-based) became very blurred. And there was still room for a collective like the Bow Gamelan Ensemble, which draws directly from Fluxus and happening traditions, to prosper and tour the world.

The British experience

Live art has certainly touched a nerve in British culture. It continues to flourish here, while in some other European countries it's lying low. There's clearly a need in society for a 'free-form' ingredient, for someone to be provocative and ask awkward questions. The anarchic character (like the American Indian 'trickster') common in many non-Western cultures fulfils this need, as does the Fool in Shakespeare. Traditional pagan rituals in Britain (like Maypoles, Guy Fawkes, sword and Morris dancing) are often pre-Christian in essence. Live artists have consciously or unconsciously often fed into these traditions. Coupled with this there's the British celebration of absurdity and eccentricity, from 'Monty Python's Flying Circus' to 'Vic Reeve's Big Night Out' on Channel 4 (which sometimes seems like a potted history of performance art clichés in itself). Bobby Baker's recent guest appearance on regional Breakfast TV was voted by viewers as one of the most popular interviews of the year. All this points to a relationship between live art and its British audience which is both complex and historically interwoven, even if they don't always recognise what they're getting.

The Carnival

by Michael McMillan

'In spite of its present status as the biggest mass street event in Europe the Notting Hill Carnival still suffers chronic underfunding and exploitation by an array of commercial interests such as the breweries, advertising agencies, London Transport, British Airways and British Tourist Board. This undermines efforts towards self-sufficiency and increases dependency on the state. Not surprisingly it is perhaps the most expressive and culturally volatile terrain on which the battle of positions between the Black community and the State are ritualised.'

'Behind the Masquerade: The Story of the Notting Hill Carnival', Kwesi Owusu & Jacob Ross, published by Arts Media Group, 1988.

In the documentation and history of performance art, carnival, much less Black artists working in interdisciplinary and mixed-media art, has been invisible or marginalised. In this book carnival is discussed not as neutral information for the practitioner, but more a mode of address to the critique of the Eurocentrism in live art. It is a critical repositioning of carnival from the realm of the exotic to that of a vital and dynamic art practice intrinsic to Black arts.

The historical and contemporary practice of carnival carries memories and aspirations of cultural political resistance, subversion, reinvention, and the celebration of emergence in the Black diaspora. It is an imaginative necessity and strategy engaging word, dance, space, image, theatre, mask (mas) in the cross-cultural psyche of modern life.

'Carnival Theatre: A Personal View', Wilson Harris in 'Masquerading: The Art of the Notting Hill Carnival', published by the Arts Council, 1986.

'The point at issue is that carnival is a medium of the multi-voiced or multi-textual spirit. Unless this is truly perceived carnival degenerates into entertainment for the sake of entertainment. And its intuitive strategy to break the polarisations tradition is forfeited in favour of an illiteracy of the imagination. It is necessary to bear this mind in a mass-media age.'

Mas is an integral part of, yet distinct from, carnival in that manifests the magic of theatre, the mystery of the mask, and the anonymity of self as signs of carnival. Mas is an abbreviation of mask and masquerade where the former is the signifier and the latter is the signified – the wearing of masks and fantastic costumes in a social gathering masquerade. The assuming of something that one was not was only a cultural political strategy for resistance in carnival, but featured in all spheres of life as means of survival – the playing Anansi, the Ginal.

Masquerade, mask, playing mas in carnival has ritualistic roots in African-Caribbean culture, and in the Black diaspora. This tradition provides the subject as actor/performer, the creative cutting edge of transformation through celebration, satire, parody, subversion and transgression. This was the cutting edge of the Canboulay, as it was originally known in Trinidad, where riots in 1881 between colonial police and the 'local population' represented only the tip of the iceberg, with a host of other forms of cultural resistance towards the colonial powers. Similar festivals such as Jonokko in Jamaica, and Crop Over in Barbados were other sites of resistance and objects of suppression for the colonial powers as much as rituals and practices of Afro-Christianity, and the cutting lyrics of calypso to the music of the talking drum and the pan.

The carnival in Notting Hill emerged in a Black population centre, which in 1958 was the site of racist attacts, and the murder of the Vicentian carpenter Kelso Cochrane which resulted in riots/uprisings/revolts. Claudia Jones, a Black woman who had been exiled from the United States because of her political activities, campaigned to free Black defendants during the Notting Hill uprisings and began the first British-based Black newspaper, the West Indian Gazette. She spoke eloquently about the need to begin a celebration of affirmation for Britain's Black communities and was instrumental in setting it up the first carnival in 1965. The Notting Hill Carnival, as much as other later carnivals around, began as a ritual for cultural political resistance and therefore continue this historic legacy.

This very condensed history of carnival is mentioned not only to contextualise its position in Britain, but to draw a thread between its tradition and modernity. As an essentially Black, yet culturally diverse festival on the streets of Britain, the territorial control of when and where to play mas and the freedom to 'sign off' the sound system says much about the historical struggles of the Black communities in Britain which are articulated through carnival.

Perceptions

Carnival has had an immense impact on popular culture whether through its appropriation in the three S's of multi-culturalism (samosas, saris and steelbands) or its exploitation in post-modernism. But if we examine popular cultural notions of carnival we find remnants of a colonial fantasy ranging from the racist to the liberal and including a repertoire of stereotypes from the non-threatening exotic event of jollification to a congregation of threatening 'savage' criminals. Within this spectrum carnival is perceived in terms of race relation agendas, public institutions and the police using the occasion to legitimise their policies or making empty multi-racial gestures as media photo opportunities. For many practitioners these notions leak into perceptions of carnival, not as an art practice with its own aesthetics, but another event in the race relations calendar. It is this notional perception of carnival, and Black arts, that has characterised the support from public institutions such as the Arts Council, regional arts boards and local authorities.

In others words, we find a liberal knee-jerk reaction to carnival in terms of race relations, rather than as cultural institution irreducible to any art form, yet central to the cutting edge of cultural politics and popular culture in Britain.

Giving carnival a monumental and institutional status in the context of the intervention of Black arts and culture is crucial. Like other institutions such as Black music, this process raises live issues and questions of cultural appropriation, ownership and equity. But dealing with carnival's workings as a kind of monolithic institution serves as a point of departure. We need to explore different approaches to carnival practice and aesthetic, which bring in other mixed-media and arts forms, and tend to break the traditionalist mould.

Approaches

Theatre is a dynamic element of carnival. 'The Man Who Lit Up The World', by Battimamzel Productions, uses theatre, mas making, design, music, dance in carnival as an interdisciplinary cultural practice. Set in a mas camp it follows the struggle of carnival mas makers who are inspired by Black inventors such as Lewis Latimer, who developed the electric light bulb for Edison and directed the introduction of early electric lighting to the UK in 1880.

Other approaches use carnival arts in a mixed-media and performance orientated context, reaching the wide audiences of carnival and festivals, as well as exhibition installations, performance art, theatre and dance. There are many practitioners who design and make mas for the Notting Hill Carnival and others, national and international. Keith Khan, a sculptor, works with materials, themes and concepts in and beyond carnival. He argues for carnival being able to question itself, not only through its position at the cutting edge of society, but to subvert its traditionalist blindness. His production 'Flying Costumes, Floating Tombs' is an integration of Caribbean festival arts, dance, movement, music, drama and speech patterns.

The piece was presented in a choreographed dramatic and abbreviated narrative form which crosses the borders of dance and drama. As its starting point it uses the Hosay Festival, a procession held in 1850 in Trinidad though its Islamic origins mourn the tragedy of Husain and Hassan, sons of the prophet Mohammed: Hassan was poisoned and Husain and his supporters were killed in the Karbala desert. Incidents from Husain's life and the tragedy at Karbala have become part of the dramatic cycle of the Hosay Festival. 'Flying Costumes, Floating Tombs' developed this even further with the 1884 uprising in Trinidad when an ordinance was passed by the colonialists to ban Hosay from public roads. Symbolising the voice of the East Indians, the colonialists feared the festival could threaten law and order and their rule. The sacrifice of Husain and Hassan paralleled the experiences of East Indian labourers in Trinidad who saw their African brothers and sisters die on board ships or on plantations. Suppression of the Hosay Festival in Trinidad parallels that of carnival festivals all over the Caribbean.

The above two productions and examples of practice, while attempting to cross the familiar visual and performing arts divide by integrating conventional theatre with carnival arts, also registers the polyphonic and irreducible nature of Black culture and arts practice.

Future potential

This has merely scratched the surface of carnival's aesthetic and practice in exploring its cultural political context. We have not dealt with the intrinsic element and sister of carnival – calypso – whose roots in the tradition of the spoken word in African culture have come full circle with the ever-increasing mainstream position of Rap/Dee Jay/MC lyrics in popular culture. Nor have we dealt with calypso's younger sister, soca which blends calypso and popular forms of Black music, and like calypso is the life blood of carnival setting its tone and rhythm – no calypso, no carnival!

In the context of Britain, we have not explored the importance of sound system culture, which through carnival's history in this country has added a cutting edge to its site of cultural political contestation.

I have attempted to briefly raise questions about the repositioning of carnival from the realm of the exotic – which speaks volumes about the relationship between Black arts and the art establishment. If live art's history has been characterised as challenges to the canonised notion of singular art form practice in Europe, then carnival poses a radical critique of the Eurocentricity of live art. As one writer recently commented, because carnival is a site of cultural political contestation – a ritualised form of resistance for Britain's Black communities – it can be seen as retaining the subvertive and critical edge, as opposed to what one designer termed its 'Butterfly Tradition' in Trinidad, where its mainstream status has achieved a touristic and acceptable image. Obviously the potential of carnival in the space of live art is yet to be revealed, but definitely on the horizon.

From dance to live art

by François Sergy

I always wanted to be a dancer. I don't know exactly why, maybe the image of the 'ballerina', the 'ideal' woman, appealed to me but I also loved moving and being creative. However as soon as I started ballet I was told I had the 'wrong' body (I was then 11!). I fought long and hard to fit in, the tougher the rejection the stronger my determination. At 17 I became involved in left-wing politics and decided a contemporary art form would be more relevant to my experience and my political commitment. I then came to England from Switzerland to study at the London Contemporary Dance School. The first year went well but soon after I was told yet again I had the wrong body! I left after three years feeling a total reject.

My love of dance survived, my politics shifted towards feminism and I became involved in 'New Dance' and martial arts (T'ai Chi, Aikido). The mid-eighties were the heydays of the Dartington Dance Festivals organised by Mary Fulkerson, who was a member of the Judson Church improvisation collective in the United States before coming to Dartington College and developing a post-modern dance course based on release work and contact-improvisation. This New Dance movement grew with

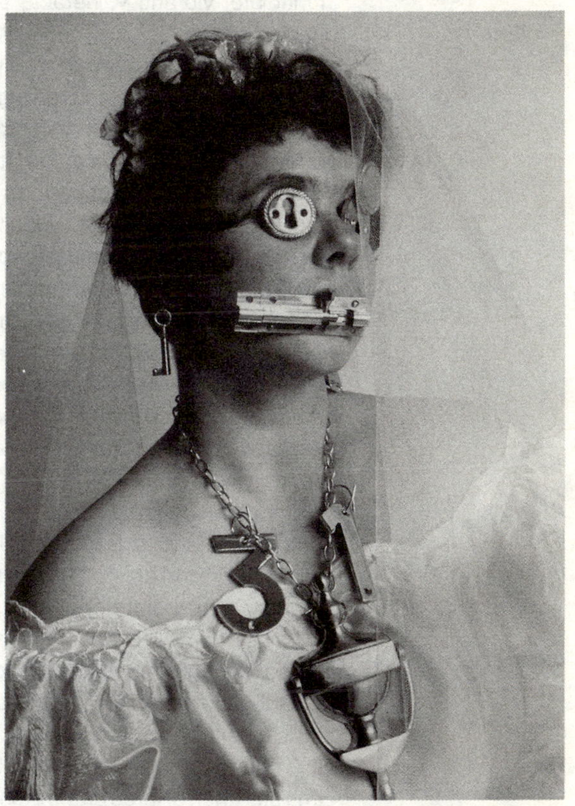

Gold, Françoise Sergy.
Photo: *Rosy Martin*

artists working collaboratively and across artforms, often in close partnership with visual artists and musicians, experimenting, pushing the boundaries of dance and creating new performance structures and a new public which was encouraged to participate. Divisions between professionals and amateurs were rejected, everyone was developing their own artistic language, some people worked collectively. New venues in disused warehouses (such as X6 Dance Space, later to become Chisenhale Dance Space) and church halls sprang up all over the place. The magazine 'New Dance' which was produced collectively remained for years the only written record of many of the events taking place and its open contributions policy made it a genuine forum of ideas and initiatives. Among the many performances in the early eighties I particularly remember the work of Maedée Duprès, Yolande Snaith and the improvised performances of Kirstie Simson, Steve Paxton and Julyen Hamilton, which were stripped of all artificial theatricality, totally immediate, vibrant, vulnerable and yet so subtle and bursting with physical daring.

New Dance allowed me finally to accept my body as it was and gave me the tools to start creating my own work. It seemed paramount at the time that I remain in control of the creative process and that I perform my own work rather than someone else's choreography. Working alone led me to perform with props such as my bicycle and a giant knitted body puppet. I was beginning to absorb aesthetically my own feminist principles and the work of many women artists inspired me to question my role as a performer, as well as the nature of performance itself. I will never forget Rose English's 'Plato's Chair' at the Bracknell Performance Festival: it was a revelation! A performance negating all performance, a mad philosophy seminar, an incredible interaction with the audience, with Rose shouting *'no, no, NO, NO!'* to a bewildered public trying to escape and being coaxed into staying, deliberately, desperately, totally convincingly.

I then began a series of collaborations with women artists and photographers (Gail Bourgeois, Honey Salvadori, Rosy Martin) and I joined the Brixton Artists Collective, a large group of artists which rented a gallery in the centre of Brixton and organised 12 exhibitions a year, including many live art events. Within the collective were several independent groups representing separate interests: Women's Work Collective, Lesbian and Gay artists, Black artists, Polish artists, sculptors, textile artists, photographers, etc. The project was initially funded by the GLC before being taken on by GLA and Lambeth Council. The gallery consisted then of three damp arches underneath the railway station. We had to do everything ourselves, administration, artistic policy, setting up the exhibitions, marketing – I gained a tremendous sense of confidence and many useful skills which encouraged me to approach more established venues and later to take off on my own. Such artist-run venues really allow artists to do things our own way, to be creatively independent and at times extremely visible. Obviously now that funding is so much more difficult to obtain, such ventures are harder to set up, particularly those committed to women or Black art.

My involvement with Brixton Artists has had a strong influence on my work. There I felt totally accepted among fellow artists with many different views and ways of sharing a commitment to art that I strongly identified with. I was a dancer, more welcomed by artists than by other dancers. My work was beginning to integrate installation, photography and dance. Where did it fit in? It wasn't 'pure' dance enough to receive funding from dance organisations and yet my very background in dance somehow put me aside of the elusive networks of the live art world. There at last were people who accepted my difference, as I accepted theirs, and my work was able to take off in directions I could never possibly have imagined before.

The venues most responsive to my work have been regional arts centres, museums and art galleries, colleges and specialist venues such as women's exhibitions. I have had least support from the promoters specifically dealing with live art or dance. Why is it that out-of-the-way places are prepared to take a weird feminist one-woman show, when the venues with a policy of experimental art turn it down? Obviously some of these venues have a higher profile and hence choose more established artists but there is another problem: such venues are few and they are run by a handful of individuals, who together form a monopoly of taste and aesthetic judgement. Decisions vital to the future of live art and affecting every artist in terms of funding and recognition are made by a tiny proportion of individual. Worse still this network controls many of the channels for performing abroad. Which is why I feel it's so important for artists to set up our own projects and venues, so we can create more opportunities for ourselves and in the long run bypass the existing networks and create new ones. For me right now this means pursuing regional funding and setting up residencies combining my own work with projects with local people/students. Over the years I have been amazed to find out how much interest there is for this kind of work, sometimes from people with little or no experience of it. I can only hope the trend will keep growing that way and the immense diversity actually present in live art will be encouraged rather than stifled.

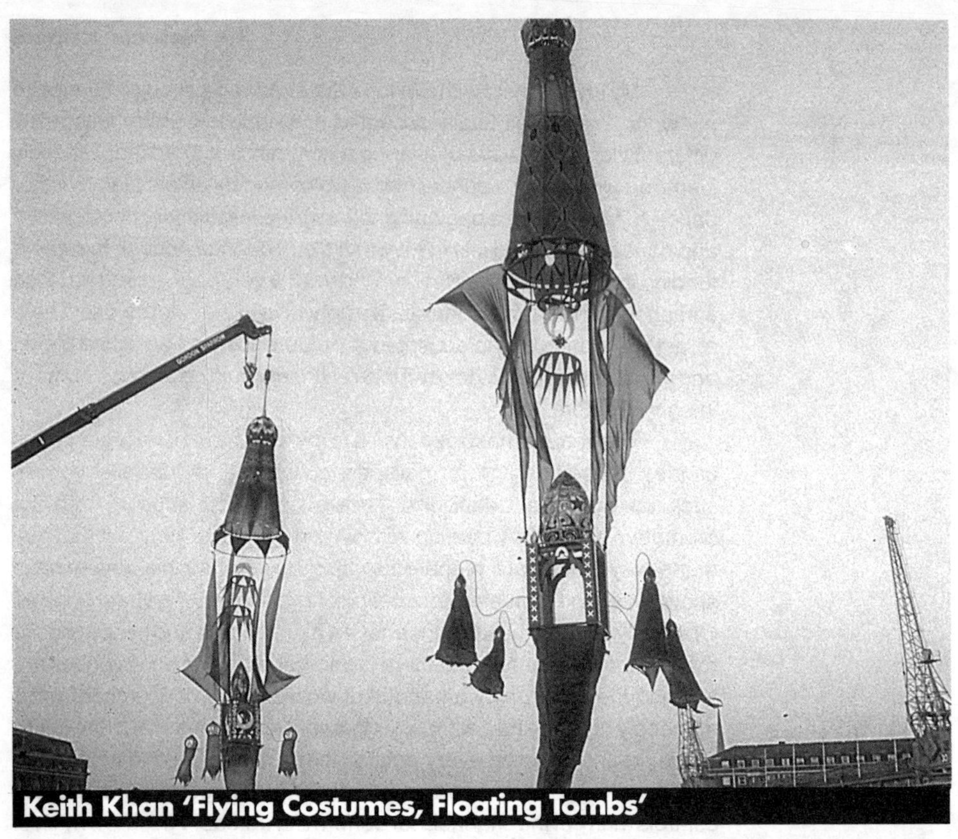

Keith Khan 'Flying Costumes, Floating Tombs'

Carnival, and the object-making, costumes and performances that I produce are, I suppose, time based. Working as a shared activity with a social function is derived from 'Mas Camps,' which are integral within carnival culture. The contribution of others is fundamental, and the most fruitful collaborations have occured with the participation of other artists (particularly other Black artists such as Ali Zaidi, Nina Edge or Betty Vaughan-Richards). The creation process is as exciting as the end performance.

'Flying Costumes, Floating Tombs' (researched by ArtAngel, commissioned by Arnolfini Live and LIFT) was a sequence of collaborations with individuals and organisations. As well as about 40 people who helped by dropping into the gallery during pre-production, there were two sets of performers – 152 in each city – that worked with the company of dancers and the choreographer, 'H' Patten. The result was a fusion of dance and powerful visuals that commemorated martyrs, killed in the Carribean and at the Jihad at Karbala.

Like most events I have made, this was meant to be seen on a variety of levels: from reflecting a diversity of cultural experiences; to the pure pleasure of lots of fabric, glitter and colour; to that of us asserting our role in the UK today.

Photo: Ali Mehdi Zaidi

4 • Learning the hard way

Sometimes things go wrong.

Live artists often take pride in the contributions they can make to a changing world. They talk of being 'at the cutting edge'. What most of us learn the hard way is that while such attitudes might seem heroic when they are being talked about, their reality can be cold and bitter and heart breaking. At the cutting edge it is too often the artist that gets cut.

The health or otherwise of live art, and how it is treated by institutions, the media and audiences, are measures of the capacity of our culture to adapt and develop.
Lois Keidan, ACGB Live Art Srategy discussion paper, 1991.

It is understandable that SuAndi embarked upon a performance residency with a fair expectation that it would succeed: her host was one of the country's major polytechnics, and the residency was funded and supported by the Arts Council of Great Britain. But SuAndi's account of the residency makes alarming reading, and the lessons that we might draw from her experience are several. First, we ought to remember that precisely because live art is 'challenging' it is often far more difficult to accommodate than many other activities, including most other art forms. SuAndi was certainly not alone in her realisation that for its promoters, her hosts, live art is often more attractive in the planning than in the actuality. Second, she made the mistake many of us might have made in such unsympathetic and apparently impenetrable circumstances: when things started to go wrong she hesitated to identify where the fault lay, and imagined – if only briefly – that the failing was hers. Among artists this is an understandable enough mistake. Working as an artist of any sort in Britain in the 1990s needs a good deal of optimism, of confidence in the face of scepticism. Often we feel we have something to prove. Live artists in particular are an ambitious breed. We set our sights high, we talk about changing the world, we often deal in the business of delight and amazement. As a consequence, we tend to imagine it is us who are letting people down when things start to go wrong. We try harder.

When SuAndi's hosts did not respond to her questions about other Black and multi-cultural work in the polytechnic – a pretty basic failing on their part – she redoubled her efforts. But, as her account of her experiences makes plain, it was already too late.

One of the recurrent themes of this book is the key importance of forward planning. Different artists put it in different ways, but the underlying lesson remains the same: it is no failure of integrity to ascertain the material feasibility of a project before you embark upon it. Indeed it is simply foolish to do otherwise. And you can do this by asking three basic questions of your project:

- Is there enough time?
- Is there enough money?
- Are there enough people (and are they the right ones)?

No matter how experienced or confident your hosts or promoters or collaborators appear, you should never assume the answers to these questions. If the answer to any of them is no, you should either try to get things improved, or you should sit down and think long and hard about whether the project is worth the heartache that it will inevitably entail.

Who am I? What am I? Where am I?

by SuAndi

You're an individual, an artist and you're on the rocky road to a nervous breakdown. Why? Because you have agreed to take a commission/ residency in live art. The journey you are about to embark on is full of trepidations and disaster. This is a statement of warning. If you think I am exaggerating, please read on.

You may shrug your shoulders at a road collision, snigger at the measles, shake your head knowingly at hangovers, emergency meetings, timetabled lectures – all those things and *much more*. But are you really prepared for the truth, the real truth of what can go wrong?

I embarked on my commission with an element of confidence. Not I might add as a live artist, this was my first sojourn into that territory, but as an artist experienced in the setting up of workshops and residencies, both for myself and others. There were things I knew I needed to know and confirm before day one.

Because this particular residency called on the skills of a Black artist, I had drawn up a list of questions on previous, if any, Black/multi-cultural input with the Polytechnic. They were never addressed. My response to this was to press onwards. This was professional suicide.

My brief was simple enough – to produce a live performance and to record both it and the developing process on video. Critical members of the public might cry 'anyone could do that'. You yourself might have just guiltily slipped that very same thought out of your mind. It isn't that simple.

This particular residency was devised to enable the artist – me, yes I still grasp desperately to that title – to develop my skills. I could do so by either creating a piece for myself or encouraging an 'interested' group of students to create their own piece.

Not being selfish by nature, well not often, I chose the latter. Anyway I had no idea how on earth I could keep a group of art students interested if they were only there to skivvy for yours truly.

The space I was initially offered had a public gallery so I rejected it. In doing so I left myself and my group in a state of homelessness. The first alternative space we were given turned out to be one earmarked for a student's degree installation and though occasionally we could work in a studio, more days than not we met and 'worked' in the students' refectory.

This resulted in the numbing of momentum and impetus to work. Each day I'd leave home that minute or two later, each arrival was awash with guilt as I found my group waiting patiently for me. I wanted to leave, opt out, I could not. Even if my own commitment was on the rapid slide to nowhere, they were becoming increasingly committed.

I had sparked their interest, stirred their curiosity, removed their doubt that I was a lunatic who waffled on continually. Slowly they were coming round to my wave length. I wasn't there to produce 'yet another' piece on racism.

There are other areas of oppression, isolation and though none of them are as harsh, in identifying them we would come to realise that no matter how corny it might sound, united we would not fall.

So there we were. Now it was a case of us and them. Us being a group of people intent on creation; and them being those who, having said they would let us play, had locked up the playground and put away all the toys.

But no matter how I tried I could no longer whip up the enthusiasm to call, or demand, more help for better rehearsal-performance-filming space. I was drowning in a sea of apologies and choking on clichés like *'it's out of my hands'*, *'I've tried everything'*.

The following are not actual quotes but they are very close to the mark: *'we never really thought this through'*, *'we never expected that you would want, needed'*, *'we've no budget left'*, *'no technician'*, *'the studio is needed (for more important things)', 'you say it's too small', 'a camera?'*

And on and on and on it went. They are not only negative and soul destroying, they are the reasons why my residency was wrapped in a suffocating blanket of stress. As an assertive person I had started the negotiations with a list of questions relating specifically to past residencies but what I had not concentrated on was the present and my future there.

Any institution runs on a number of engines. Each runs independently of the other, so independently that quite often one engine has no idea of the running power or fuel need of the other. Did I know that?

My education spanned the fifties and sixties when the head of any education building was quite simply the person in charge. No member of staff could initiate their own project without a total consultation with the office down the hall. Now I am inclined to believe all staff have to do is to present a convincing project on paper, prove that no extra cost will be incurred on the annual budget, and they are off.

My residency took place in the fine art department but needed to journey into film and video. Film and video it appeared had not been consulted. But before I even speak of the technical problems there were human ones.

My direct contact had to step back because of a family death, and I could not bring myself to tackle a grieving father. My second contact – 'best friend' – was a part-time lecturer with little power or knowledge – *'I'm not sure there is a Students Union'*. By day two I knew I was walking a tightrope, anger became my best friend and anger is so negative.

Would you like to be introduced upstairs? No, I had visited the top of the building once and met the bursar who had unwittingly boasted of a new cache of money. I had been told repeatedly that there was no money, when I was unable to list my material needs. But how could I, the piece was supposed to be a collaboration, I hadn't even met the students.

A press meeting was on the agenda by day two and anger told me to leave early. This appetite for publicity is one of the most exploitative elements for artists, brought on by self-management within education. No one asked me why I hadn't kept the appointment. No one cared. I was there, the vacancy had been filled, now I was expected to simply do my job.

I had been given an office, well a desk, it was cold and bare. For me it reflected an apathy that my cohabitees shared. They had a key, I did not, and though they were genuinely warm to me they were not linked to my work. Still, one took time to show me round the building. Up to then I had no idea where to get a coffee, a book, secretarial help, the number of buildings or campuses or how to escape from the sixth floor in an emergency. To my way of thinking these were all useful, practical pieces of information. My awareness was rising as I began to realise where I had gone wrong.

I was visible in as much there was a new face on the floor. But there was a whole bloody building who had absolutely no idea that I was there, never mind what I was doing. And if they did know of my existence they showed that knowledge by calling meetings and compulsory lectures every time I walked into the building.

Eventually tiring of this I travelled to another town, (that's when the car was hit), to negotiate a performance space and though the venue was warm and hospitable it turned out they could not accommodate our needs. So after a number of false starts we eventually managed to sneak into a theatre and film everything in one go.

It wasn't perfect, the camera from the poly was a shoddy piece of equipment, the resulting inferior film had to be binned. The students were tired, cold and hungry. But they never lost the desire to achieve.

Their commitment is something that host venues need to discover. It's not enough to waffle on about art, art, art. You have to also think about people. Artists are people and they want more than absent-minded invitations to lunch.

I have drawn up a check list. It is neither complete nor in order of priorities but it does serve as a beginning:

- Are all the necessary people/departments/organisations aware of the residency? Do not take 'yes' as an answer, demand to meet with them.
- Ask for a copy of the building's timetable to prevent you holding workshops during compulsory lectures.
- Request a plan of the building site and allow time to visit all those that are art related, otherwise you will simply be given a brief tour of studio spaces.
- Ensure that you are properly introduced to all members of staff. I held an introductory performance, the date was arranged but on the day staff were busy interviewing prospective first-years.

Also you have to remember that quite often staff are not known to each other. I witnessed a Black member of staff being mistaken for my boyfriend and had to re-introduce himself.

- Which senior member of staff will be your support, your 'best friend'?
- Which staff wish to be involved and in what capacity?
- Where will the performance take place, has a date been secured? (There was an eagerness to book the theatre but they had forgotten that the venue was needed for the degree finals).
- What are the long-term aims of the commission's contribution to the college study program? (No one actually requested to sit in on a workshop).
- Who will be responsible for technical support? (There was a vacancy during my residency).
- Who handles the petty cash? (I used my own money).

On the day we were filming a memorial service was being held for family members killed in a plane crash. A student slipped out, made her contribution, then returned to console her parents and, I have no doubt, share her own grief. Need I say more.

If this residency was anywhere close to being a success it is due to that level of involvement, the support of a good arts officer (Lois Keidan) and most of all people who have not forgotten that they are first and foremost human beings.

All I can say is thank heavens for students.

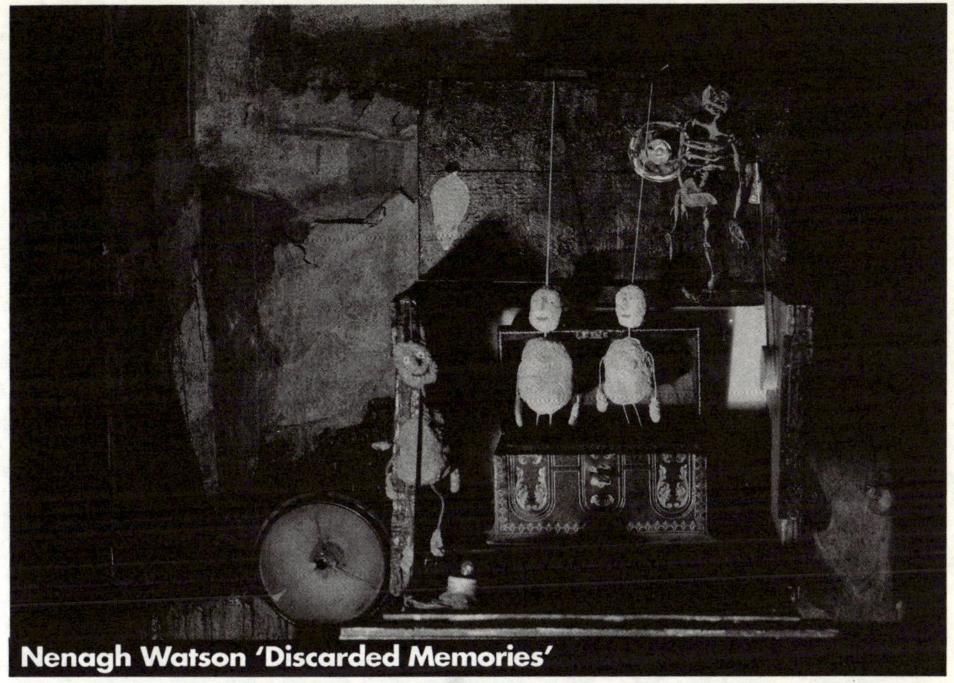

Nenagh Watson 'Discarded Memories'

For the past eight years I have combined sculpture and performance, making work that could be defined as 'theatre of objects and figures'. The majority of my work is created In collaboration with painter Rachel Field. The work is designed for a small audience (30-50 depending on seating arrangements). It demands that the audience is receptive in bringing their own thoughts and asociations, creating their own individual narrative. I want to create an intimate atmosphere and for the audience to feel involved in something extra-ordinary to be shared. I have moved away from presenting 'theatre' in terms of audience size and setting. Ideally I would like to present work to 10 people in a small space created specifically for the event.

The education unit at a City Art Gallery took 'Discarded Memories' as an extra gallery event to compliment Paolozzis 'Lost Magic Kingdoms'. Instead of presenting the work as a piece for adults, it was promoted as 'a magical puppet show' and I overheard a father of two young children ask 'when's the Punch and Judy?' only to be told by the education officer to 'come back at 11am'. These errors were made even though I had taken considerable care and time attempting to convey the nature of the work. This prejudice and misconception is carried over into the structure of networking, venues and funding.

Photo: Ann McGuinness. Nenagh Watson works as DOO COT Theatre of Objects and Figures.

5 • Audience, context, content

by Richard Layzell

There are a few very basic questions to consider when planning a performance, which are often inter-related. The medium of live art deals, in a public way, with an audience – this goes without saying. Even if the aim is only to present the work in the form of documentation, there's still an audience to be taken into account. More often than not, the relationship of performer to audience is a central issue and can determine how a work evolves.

Who are you aiming at?

You may have a particular audience in mind, passers-by in the street, for example, or an average art gallery-going public. You may choose not to be too aware of this, preferring to leave it to chance. 'Whoever turns up' may be enough. You can be sure whether you've advertised the event or not, you'll have to deal with an audience, so giving it some thought in advance will prepare you and your ideas.

The casual passer-by

My experience of this kind of audience is that they don't usually stay for long, unless you find a way of stopping them or involving, enthralling or scandalising them. There are many encounters happening on the streets of cities that are genuinely threatening or disturbing. A performance artist on the street is likely to elicit the same kind of response as a 'freak' of some kind to be avoided. This, however, may be desirable. You may want your work to be glimpsed as people pass a shop window, or seen from the top deck of a bus, or to be so much a part of everyday life that people hardly notice it.

Sure there is a confrontation, because I want the audience to react, to experience, to say 'this is crazy'. So laugh at it, or shout at it. But don't just sit there. The audience has got to work just as hard as I do. That may sound pompous, but otherwise they won't get anything out of it.

Andre Stitt

The public spectacle

The opposite approach is to take on the idea of some kind of 'spectacle' in a public place. In this case the aim would be to entice an audience, be strategically placed to draw the most attention and possibly have mounted a large-scale publicity campaign beforehand. There can be problems with teenagers heckling and jeering, but you are likely to draw a lot of attention if you're positioned in the kind of area or arena where people congregate. Every town or city has such a meeting place.

The enormous advantage of performing in a public place is that you're dealing with the kind of people who would never set foot in an art gallery or even a theatre. You have the chance of communicating your ideas to people who wouldn't normally be exposed to them and you may also gain considerable press attention. Having performed both in the street and with an invited audience, I'd say the two experiences are very, very different, not better or worse than each other. It's worth experiencing them both.

The invited audience

Whatever context you've chosen or been chosen for, whether gallery, theatre, studio or outdoor space, if your audience has been specially invited you'll be able to make certain predictions about them. If people have taken the trouble to go to a certain place at a certain time to see an event, then they have an investment in getting something out of it. They've made a commitment. This applies all the more if they've paid an admission fee. Their expectations will be very varied. They may be excited, slightly afraid and anxious, interested, cynical, wanting to be entertained, they may be supporting you as a friend, they may be completely open-minded. The main strengths of live art as a medium are its incredible breadth and this very issue – that audiences cannot predict what will happen. Anything is possible and they know this. So with an invited audience, you have their attention and probably their good-will, certainly at the start. From then on, it's up to you.

It's a generalisation, but this kind of audience is usually from a fairly narrow stratum of society, the kind of people who know about experimental art forms. The odd person may come who has never been to anything like it before, but they are the exceptions, unless you've become a household name, of course.

Cabaret & clubs

There's now an extensive network of these venues throughout Britain. If your work fits in and you enjoy the lifestyle there are plenty of opportunities, particularly in cabaret. Nightclubs are slightly more difficult and it's advisable to check out who else is on the billing. I once discovered, too late, that I was billed as the support for a reggae band. Some of the audience assumed I'd be a reggae band too. Clubs have a ready-made, often large audience, who'll be there anyway. But their expectations may not easily accommodate something that doesn't match what usually happens in clubs.

The same applies to cabaret. Most people go along to laugh, laugh, laugh. If you're offering something more thought-provoking they might give you a hard time. This may, of course, be exactly what you want to happen. These kinds of venue also make specific demands on a performer. You're likely to have a very restricted space to perform in, a very short time to set up and a short, probably 20 minutes maximum, slot for your piece. The advantage is, once again, you're reaching the kind of audience that probably wouldn't see you elsewhere and they may thoroughly welcome what you have to offer as something different from the usual stand-up comedians.

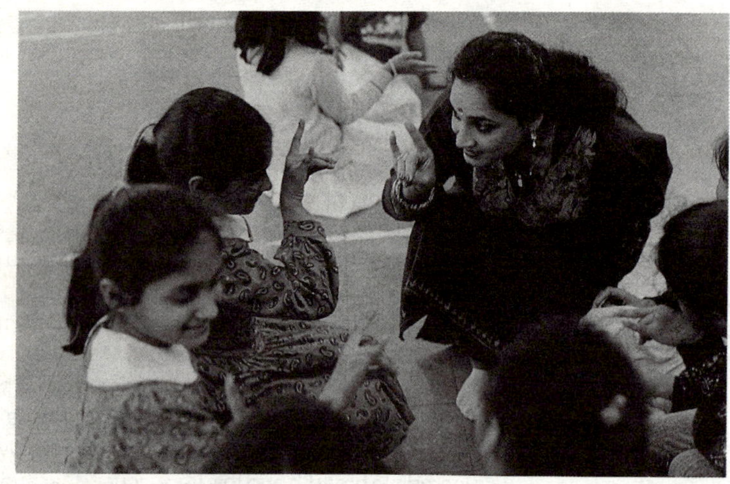

Working towards the Handsworth performance. Richard Layzell, **1988**

The target audience

It's perfectly possible to find your own audience, to choose a social group and aim your performance at them. I first came to this from a dissatisfaction with the often narrow nature of invited audiences, believing there was a wider audience out there somewhere who were quite capable of 'understanding' what I was doing. As a consequence, I began working on a piece specifically aimed at a group of ten-year-old children in Handsworth, Birmingham. The performance was about this social group and directed at them, but I saw no reason why it wouldn't communicate successfully with any group and age. This proved to be the case. So by choosing a target audience in the first place, you're not necessarily limiting the overall impact your work can have.

Context

The context, environment or 'placing' of a performance event can also condition how it develops. This includes how it's presented, in terms of promotion and publicity. Some of these considerations have already been looked at with respect to audience, but many aspects are inter-related. Here are some issues of context represented as opposite poles:

A large-scale event	...	An intimate event for small audiences
Seen in passing	...	Has to be sat through from beginning to end
Site specific (designed for one particular place)	...	Can be performed anywhere
Audience as focal point	...	Audience incidental
Conventionally seated audience	...	Unconventionally arranged audience
Political action	...	Art for art's sake
Presented/publicised for a wide audience, ie no 'art' words	...	Presented/publicised conventionally within art/theatre context
A tightly choreographed set piece	...	Highly improvised, bouncing off audience
Communicable essentially to English speakers	...	Communicable to any nationality
Part of a festival of live art, experimental theatre, etc	...	Your event is it
Within the context of a related art form, ie dance, music, film, etc	...	No framework – can't be pinned down

Some unusual contexts

Boats, trains, landscapes, mental hospitals, children's homes, restaurants, supermarkets, cinemas... you name it.

see 'Festivals', 11 • Live art promoters & 'National Events', 14 • Funding

With the trend in installations and contexts towards more and more unusual settings, like some of the above (as reflected in festivals like Edge and TSWA3D), there is the same potential for live art to move away from some of the conventions that it has evolved over the past few years. The business of even trying to define contexts for live art goes against the roots of the medium, which were concerned with breaking down and challenging convention, always searching for new contexts.

What do you want to say?

There are as many approaches to working out a piece of performance as there are artists doing it. Similarly, there are countless reasons for doing it: a natural extension of something else you're doing; the only area left for you to express yourself in; an experiment; a risk; you've always done it without realising; you see someone else and become inspired; you get commissioned, put in a proposal and it gets accepted; a friend or colleague asks you to join them; you think you might get famous fast; you simply want to give it a try; and so on.

If you're coming to it from another discipline, another art form, then you already have something to work from as a starting point. For example, if you're a painter, then your first performance piece could be very, very visual, with just a small amount of live action, text, sound or whatever. If you're a dancer, the piece could be mainly movement-based, but might include some spoken text and might go against your own conventions of what dance is, or should be. This raises again the fundamental issue that the whole area of live art has evolved around: it does not follow convention. It continues to change direction and re-define itself. It's wide open. It's subversive. Anything is possible. It can be about anything. It can take any form. The only limitation, if you can call it that, is that something happens over a period of time and there is an audience involved in some way.

I stress this as a reminder that whatever the imaginary boundaries or barriers may be, they can be challenged. Another, slightly more conventional way of looking at it is that live art is the meeting ground of all the other art forms, the grey area where a great deal of experimentation and cross-fertilisation goes on.

The emphasis can be on: visual, verbal, aural and movement in varying degrees. Taking any one of these, say 'aural' and using it as a starting point, you could break it down further, using musical terminology, into for example: repeated theme, crescendo, rhythm and raga, giving possible structures or concepts to use in a performance that may have no music in it whatsoever. Similarly, you could choose a poem, a political/social issue, an object, a photograph, an atmosphere, a memory, as a starting point and then begin to break it down, re-structure it, add to it, relate it to something opposite, involve the audience in an unusual way, and so on. This only represents one way of proceeding. I can deal with some areas of consideration in greater detail, but thankfully there'll always be more.

Ritual

Life is full of everyday rituals we take for granted. If you place one, eg cleaning your teeth or reading a paper, in an unfamiliar context, it takes on a different meaning. It becomes material to be de-constructed, repeated, enlarged, whatever. Within a performance, the most banal everyday action tends to take on a deeper significance. There's been a tradition of 'performance as ritual' and all that it implies, which may open up an approach you hadn't considered. Although the risk here is to produce a closed ritual performance that excludes the audience. Your actions may have a symbolic and highly personal meaning for you, but can your audience understand these meanings and do you want them to?

Self-indulgence

Many performers have chosen to deal with autobiography as a starting point, or as the central core of their work. This, combined with the often bizarre forms that performances can take, has led to the stereotyped view of live art as being self-indulgent. The stereotype probably involves nudity, a man with a bucket on his head, some feathers, a candle, no-one able to make sense of it, that kind of thing. Like all stereotypes, it doesn't mean a lot, but we're stuck with it until there's a shift in understanding. I believe the label of 'self-indulgence' is not only damning, but also inaccurate. The same criticism could be applied to a lot of visual art, but the difference is that the audience can pass it by so quickly. With performances you're stuck there, bored, confused or irritated, sometimes you're not making an effort to involve yourself in the work and sometimes you simply don't like it. It would be more accurate and honest to say you don't like a performance than to accuse it of self-indulgence.

For the performer, the implication is that your work is not communicating enough or it's boring. Do you want to communicate your ideas more clearly? Do you want it to be boring?

Timing

If you've not performed before it's hard to understand the significance of timing, unless you have an innate sense of it. The main pitfall is thinking your piece is interesting to the audience because you find it interesting to perform. This doesn't follow. Performing is certainly interesting and exciting. It's a dynamic, highly charged and frightening experience. You're likely to feel on edge and very engaged in what you're doing. If each member of the audience was up there with you, they'd feel the same way, but they're not. They're sitting or standing, fairly rooted, unless you've decided to involve them in some way. Try to imagine yourself in their shoes. Would this sequence work from their point of view, not yours? A five minute piece can be more memorable than a 90 minute epic.

To gain some clues about timing you could either attend workshops in performance skills, rehearse your work or look at yourself on video, but make sure they are appropriate for you. Personally, I find rehearsals very difficult. I need an audience to bounce off. I let the work evolve audience by audience. But that's me.

see 'Training', 6 • Starting out

Feedback

It's often very hard to be objective about how a performance has gone. Feedback from the audience can be very useful. If *everyone* you speak to makes the same comment, positive or negative, ie it's too long, or the beginning was a complete surprise, you can be sure that this is how it's coming across. If you want it to feel long, then fine. If you don't, then change it.

Improvisation

From the success of improvised comedy in Britain at the moment, it's easy to see the appeal and magic of improvisation. If the audience isn't in a position to know whether you're improvising or not, then there's a different set of rules which you can operate freely, sometimes directly engaging the audience in 'real time', sometimes telling your pre-planned 'story' in whatever form it takes. Improvisation doesn't suit everyone, but it's there if you want to try it.

Props/objects

These can be a crucial aspect and spark off ideas for the performance itself. People with a visual art training will know all about this. It's often how first experiments in performance happen. A painting, sculpture or construction suggests a *live* element to enhance or extend it. And, of course, these are some of the origins of this art form. 'Happenings' in the '50s & '60s occurred partly for these reasons.

Collaboration

Working with other people can be very supportive, practically and emotionally. It can be a way of getting started and of moving forward if you're stuck. It can open up new possibilities and challenges that only other people can bring. Collaboration can take many forms. It can range from asking someone to sit in at a rehearsal to give feedback and advice, to a large-scale production with several performers where all creative decisions are made collectively. Collaborators can be fellow artists/performers, children, writers, musicians, designers, scientists, gardeners.... Don't underestimate the creativity in others.

How ideas develop

I'd like to give some examples from my own work, illustrating how many issues can come into play when developing ideas for a performance. I've chosen three recent pieces, which each had a different kind of starting point.

'Move the Rabbit' began with a clear image in my mind of a man with a pale face in a dark suit and also a desire for an ecological theme. It would be spare and intense. It was about all I started with. The next stage was to take some black and white slides of fallen trees. This was just after the storm in 1987 and I didn't know how these slides would fit in, but was aiming to work intuitively. The way these separate starting points knitted together happened gradually over subsequent weeks. A few spoken words began to develop; an audio tape with text, linking a dream state to the storm; a doctored dark suit, re-designed to suggest an animal quality. Most of all, it evolved through performing it. The first performance was about 50% improvised. Subsequent performances much less so. It still changes slightly, but now has a defined structure and sequence of events which are constant. My collaborator in this piece was Colin Watkeys from the Finborough Theatre Club, where it was first performed. He gave invaluable feedback and support with an idea which I had very little confidence in at first.

'Gravity' started in response to the experience of acting in a film called 'Vernissage'. I played the central character, a sculptor having his first exhibition for ten years, in a smart gallery. It was the first time I'd

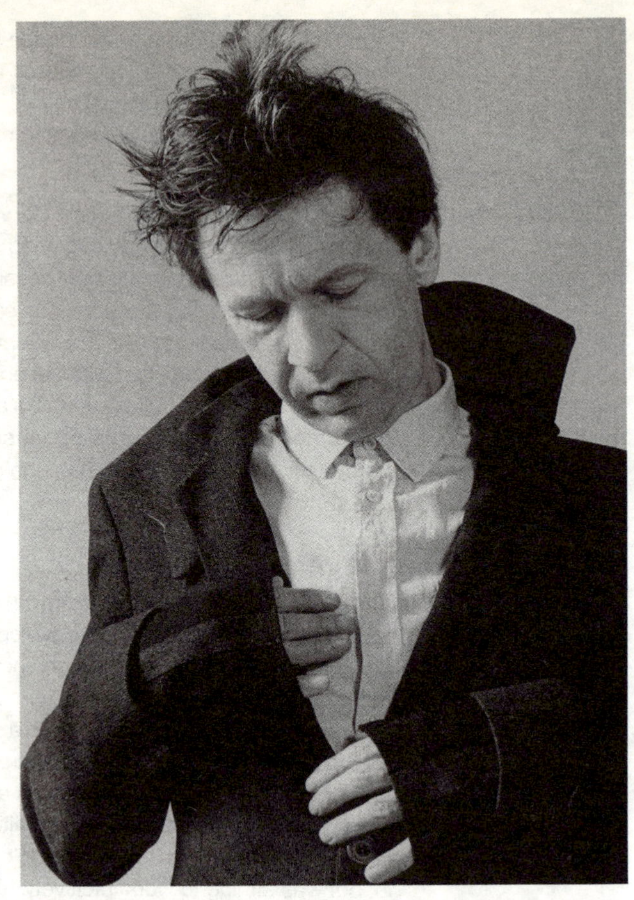

Move the Rabbit,
Richard Layzell, **1987.**
Photo: *Honey Salvadori*

performed in a film. The director was Oskar Jonasson, a student at the National Film School. There was a certain amount of collaboration and there were a lot of parallels with my own life. At times I began to wonder if the film was about me or the fictional character I was portraying. I found the experience so strange I decided to do an improvised performance based on it. There would be many levels of reality. I would take on several roles – film director, myself, sculptor, gallery owner, the sculpture. It started as 90% improvisation and continues to evolve and change, depending on context and audience. Now it's about 30% improvised. There's a lot of autobiography in the piece and the audience is often left wondering what is truth and what is fiction.

'The Revolution – You're In It!' was commissioned as an out of gallery event by Kettles Yard Gallery in 1989. It was timed to coincide with the Cambridge Festival and an exhibition at Kettles Yard on the theme of revolution. Initial meetings to discuss the project took place about six months before it was due to start, so there was a considerable time to plan it out, almost like a campaign. From the start it was to be a performance aimed at a wide audience, in fact, if possible the whole population of Cambridge. Linking into the theme of revolution, I decided to take the standpoint that we in Britain were in a state of revolution,

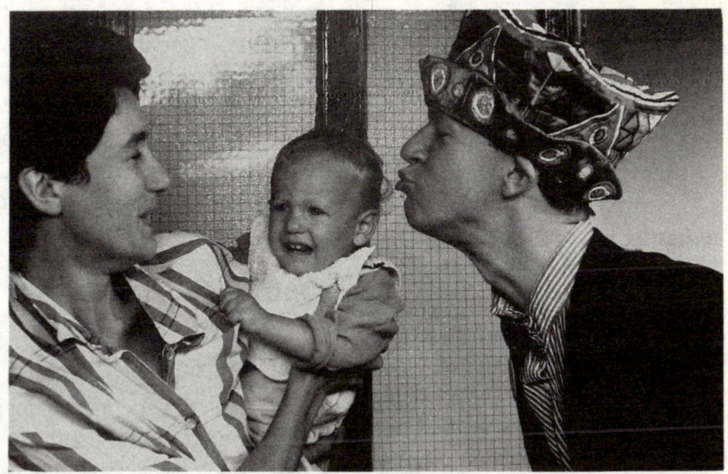

***The Revolution – You're In It!* Bailey Savage in action.** Richard Layzell, **1989**

under Thatcherism. I would adopt the persona of a successful product of the Thatcher years, a businessman who has prospered tremendously over the past decade. I would take to the streets of Cambridge encouraging people to celebrate our revolution.

At the time I had an Irish artist, Trevor Cromie, assisting me on an Arts Council placement, so we developed the piece together. We came up with the name of 'Bailey Savage' as hitting the mark and began planning a series of events spanning the two weeks in which the performance would take place. These included tree planting, greeting the work-force, appearing daily on local radio, public speaking, launching a cocktail, impromptu appearances in pubs and on the street and, most important of all, driving around in a large car. The car would add credibility to this public figure and make the performance very mobile. I saw the car as a moving sculpture, a portable context, a businessman's outer casing. Bailey would be arrogant, loud, unable to listen, domineering, obnoxious and basically mad, somewhere between a politician and a religious fanatic. Meeting him on the street would not be a pleasant experience.

With this work, the context was central to how the ideas took shape. In all the publicity material my real name wasn't mentioned, nor was the word 'art' or 'performance'. It was intended that the audience would have to work out for themselves whether I was for real or not, and if not, why I was doing this.

I've subsequently performed a version of this piece for an invited audience in theatres and galleries, but it doesn't have the same edge. It was designed for the street and that's where it works best. Apart from Trevor Cromie, the other crucial collaborator was Hilary Gresty from Kettles Yard. Her particular viewpoint as curator and organiser gave a quite different perception and because of the nature of the project she was able to be much more involved than with a more conventional performance.

Inevitably, if you are working within the field of New Work (whether it's music, performance or art), you will come across people who cannot and will not appreciate the value of your work. If your work is in any way useful, however, you will also meet people whose enthusiasm, encouragement and interest spur you on to take greater risks and reach for higher goals. It is those people who I remember when things are not going quite as I'd like them to.

Claire Spafford: Glory what Glory

Some final thoughts

A few words of encouragement if you're starting out:

- be prepared to take risks
- use friends for support and feedback
- expect post-performance deflation – it passes
- try to keep clear about your intentions
- keep together, parallel activities going
- don't be easily put off
- it's OK to enjoy yourself.

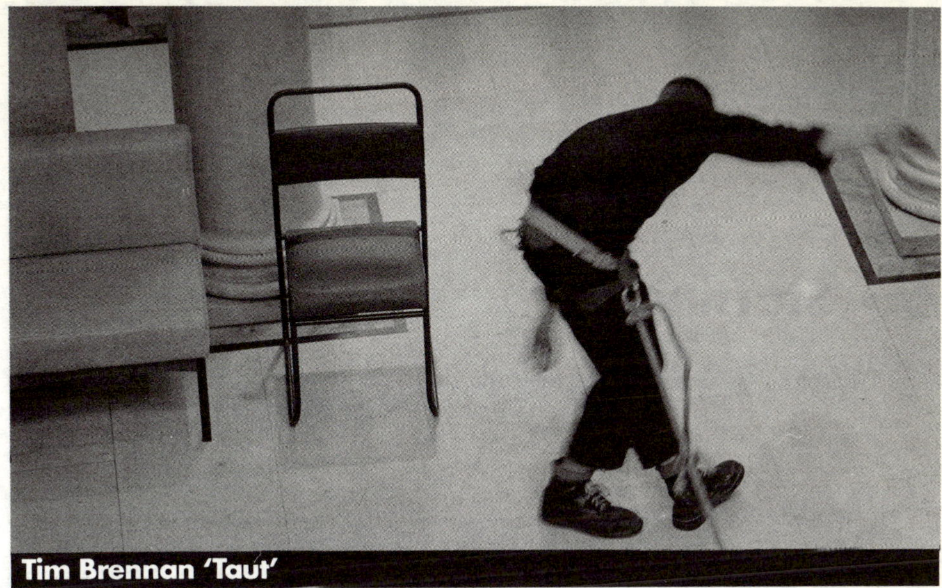

Tim Brennan 'Taut'

My live work was a direct development of my interest and work in sculpture. I see live art as a sculptural activity that dispenses with the traditional role of the artefact . I began working in performance when I realised that the static object relegated the element of risk in cultural activity. It is the risk, that leaves the performer/artist open to the collective intervention of the viewer or the unforeseen event, that interests me. The 'audience' or 'viewer' is important in my work for a number of reasons:

- The 'viewer' constitutes a witness within the work. Without a witness the work would not exist as performance behaviour, but would assert itself purely as documentation or as myth.
- My work at times concerns itself with the psychological relationship between myself and the viewer. For this reason the viewer is treated as material within the work.
- The viewer can intervene within my work. This is important because it questions the notion of authorship and provides a structure where the orientation of meaning can be collectively altered within a work.

The shift from what could be described as a consensual form of government, resulting from the adoption of monetarist policies has restricted the development of those cultural projects initiated in the early seventies, that questioned the division between art and life. In effect what government policy now requires is a definitive concept of performance which falls within the realm of theatre and spectacle (broadly popularist entertainments) or consists of some form of packaged artefacts (mimicking production for the market).

Photo: Simon Drury. 'Taut' was performed with John Wilson at Ferens Art Gallery, 1988

6 • Starting out

by Ann Cullis

Start small. You could do a lot worse. For most of us it is best to start small, since mistakes and disasters on this scale are easier to deal with, as are the finances involved.

Communication

Unless you start somewhere, you will never know whether your ideas work as live art. It could be that, having experimented, you find live art is not the best way to say what you want to say – in which case, stop! But at least you will have found out.

Audience reactions are the best way to gauge whether you are communicating what you intended. To communicate, you need to be articulate in your chosen language – live art.

Hard work

Working in this area is not an easy option: you need to be as good a technician for live art as you do for sculpture or painting. In fact you need to be a better technician because you are working with some very dangerous, unpredictable and exciting media: time and people.

Most artists who work in live art would say it is hard work of a quite different kind to studio work, closer in kind to that of a dancer or actor because of the physical and mental demands you must make on yourself to succeed.

How some have started

Many artists working in live art have come out of art college. The boundaries between live art and other more traditional media are often very blurred, as is the definition of 'live art' itself. Some artists start to experiment with live art whilst at college, others wait until they have assimilated their training and thought about how they can use or reject it.

> **I began working in 'performance-as-art' in 1983 because I was unimpressed with the manner of performing I had witnessed.... I wanted to find out if I could do better. I wanted to do better.**
>
> a. x. fraser

Richard Nicolson was on a fine art course at Leicester Polytechnic working in the area between painting and sculpture. His interests in painted constructions and environments led him to start live work during his final year. Friends formed an ad hoc 'company' to put on performances of 'Small Traffic' (1983) in his studio area for fellow students and friends.

The Nottingham Feminist Art Group in the early eighties was a thriving group who put on many performance evenings in the old Midland Group building in Nottingham city centre. This was a period when it was probably easier and relatively cheaper to book venues for small scale events.

Concrete Creations in Birmingham are a partnership who make public art works and interventions ('creativity in the concrete jungle'), often on commission through building up contacts.

There are almost as many ways of starting out as there are ideas and artists. Below are some of the routes artists often pursue.

Formal training opportunities

Whether or not you can be 'trained' in live art is debatable, and whether or not it is training provided by art colleges even more so.

There are certain skills and techniques which can be learnt in order to become a competent painter or sculptor, but for the artist these are not so obvious. However you will find that the general training at art college will always be useful (even if only to kick against), teaching you a visual language and the ability to observe accurately and to experiment with ideas in a creative way.

Groundwork

Dancers learn classroom exercises to develop technique and stamina. They do not perform them on stage, yet they inform every movement that they make when they dance. In the same way the training of artists at college is an excellent basis for live art.

Formal training opportunities in live art are few. It will depend very largely on the college and probably even more on individual lecturers and their interests. Often colleges, particularly the more traditional ones, are overtly unsympathetic to any art that cannot be framed and put on a wall.

Difficulties at college

Experimentation and non-traditional work are not always encouraged. You may find that whilst in theory you are at college to be creative and adventurous, in practice the opposite is the case. This is especially true when it comes to assessments and degree shows. Presenting live art as part of a degree show is risky and success depends on the assessor, so it is a good idea to find out their interests.

However, there are a number of institutions where the enthusiasm of individuals has meant that an atmosphere sympathetic to live art has developed. The most notable examples are Richard Layzell at Wimbledon School of Art, Fran Hegarty at Sheffield Polytechnic, Stuart Brisley at the Slade, Monica Ross at Central/St Martins, Anthony Howell and Mona Hatoum at Cardiff, Alastair Maclennan at the University of Ulster, Rose Garrard at Dartington, and Chris Wainwright at Newcastle Polytechnic. In some cases their influence has been limited to specific courses, with other courses within the same college remaining immune; in other cases, these people have risen to positions of some seniority within their institutions. In two polytechnics it is virtually possible to follow a degree course majoring in live art: at Leicester Polytechnic, Jo Scanlan has expanded her interest in non-text-based performance into a main component of the Creative Arts degree; and perhaps most obviously at Nottingham Polytechnic the Department of Visual Arts is headed by Robert Ayers and offers opportunities to students with an interest in live art on its courses in Fine Art, Theatre Design, and – most specifically – Creative Arts.

Informal training opportunities

Other getting-started opportunities are available if you keep your eyes open.

Workshops

Welfare State International run residential summer courses on aspects of their particular brand of live art activity. In recent years, a number of promoters and venues have organised training courses of one sort or another led by experienced live artists. These have included The Quarter Club/Green Room, Manchester (in 1987) and South Hill Park, Bracknell (in 1989). Despite the success of these events, there seems to be an absence of activity in this area at present, but with the gradual move of polytechnics and colleges into summer-school work, we may well see them taking over this important role.

These can sometimes be quite expensive and it is worth investigating funding from your regional arts board (RAB). However, you will need to convince the visual arts officer that this is something

see 20 • Contacts

worthwhile, and you will probably have to fill in a fairly complex form about why you want to do this workshop/course, how it will benefit you and how it will benefit your RAB.

Start local

Another route, as mentioned at the beginning, is more or less to train yourself by simply starting on a small scale to make public performances or events. Economy will be essential so don't be over-ambitious. On the other hand much live art is produced on a shoestring.

Local studio groups usually have annual exhibitions which often include public events such as opening studios for a weekend or putting on workshops. These are good opportunities to introduce your work to a wider audience while keeping it on manageable scale.

But generally, opportunities are there because you make them happen.

Performance platforms

Established by the late Steve Rogers at the Midland Group Arts Centre in Nottingham in 1980, the 'Performance Art Platform' became an annual event and grew into one of the most important institutions to sustain livo art activity in this country. It combined work by established artists, including a few big 'names', with work by unknowns and those new to performance. It blossomed into the 'National Review of Live Art' under the care of Nikki Millican who, on the financial collapse of the Midland Group in 1986 took it first to the Riverside Studios in London, and then to the Third Eye Centre in Glasgow. Once again it is threatened by the financial fragility of its host venue but it seems unthinkable that such a mainstay of live art activity will not overcome the centre's recent financial demise. Latest reports suggest the event will be staged biennially and become the 'International Review'.

During about the same period that the 'National Review of Live Art' has thrived, there have been a number of festival-type events staged by and for students. Colleges in Coventry, Hull and Sheffield have hosted these on one or more occasions. The most recent was the 'Expo' festival organised by Emma Ghafur in Nottingham in the summer of 1991. This was intended specifically for students and graduates of the country's various creative arts and performing arts courses. There seems a strong possibility that 'Expo' will secure its future by becoming the 'platform' component of Nottingham's 'Contemporary Archives' festival.

Most 'platform' events invite submissions from would-be participants. Like open exhibitions, work is selected by a panel of artists and critics whose names are announced beforehand. Competition is sharp so be prepared for disappointment.

Preparation
Think about your platform submission. What is it about your work that makes it stand out? Why should they accept you and not someone else? Applications of this kind are good for making you consider what you are doing, and why. If you don't know, no-one else will.

Questions to ask
Remember too that a platform is a public event. If previously you have only shown your work to fellow students and friends, you may need to consider the audience who will see it (who they are, what their experiences and expectations will be), the space in which your work will be seen, the time of day or position in the programme (will it be the last item at the end of a long day when everyone is desperate to get to the bar?) Any of these things might require you to modify your work in some way.

see 5 • Audience, context, content

Large mixed shows such as 'New Contemporaries' are also possibilities but, again, success depends very much on who the selectors are.

Getting involved

The more contacts you make the better.

Contacts
With contacts you will be able to find venues, money, people who can print cheap publicity, find sources of free scrap metal, play unusual musical instruments – whatever you need for your live art work.

Work hard making contacts and determination will bring rewards! It may take a while but stick at it. Get involved in your local art 'scene' generally. If there is a studio group or artists' organisation in your area, join it. If your local gallery needs invigilators or helpers at private views, do it.

The pay-off
You will get fed up doing work for nothing but in the long-term it does pay off because you will have met so many people and, more importantly, they will have met you: you will become someone whom people think of, someone who gets involved.

Self-publicity

While you are doing all this, you can look for interesting people, buildings, materials which you can use in your live art work. Tell people about your ideas and continue to make live art. The worst thing is to spend a whole year planning the live art event of the decade which never happens. Much better to do some workshops for local schools or community groups to develop your ideas – and maybe even get paid too.

Flexibility does not come naturally. It is hard work for most of us. But in an increasingly competitive art world where everyone is chasing the same scarce funding, it is your most valuable skill.

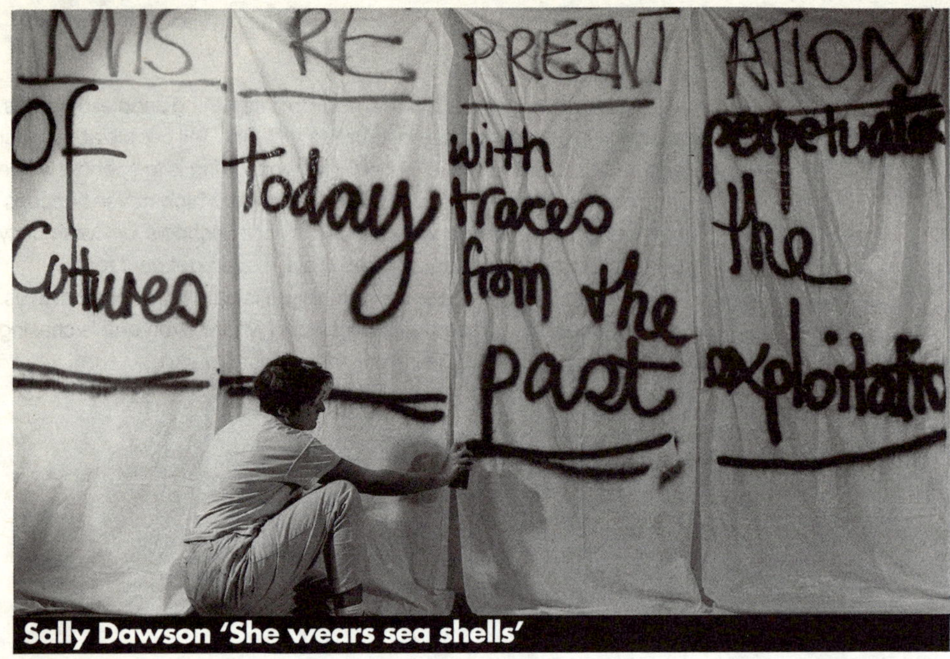

Sally Dawson 'She wears sea shells'

I found out about 'performance art' myself really, with a bit of advice, at art college. I read, researched and rooted out information on live art and got visiting lecturers and performers to provide as broad a base framework as possible. About this time I became aware of and active in feminist politics, and started using live art as a means of communicating ideas from a feminist perspective.

As a feminist I see live art as being an important and exciting method of expression, because you are visible as a performer and have an immediate relationship with your audiences. Having worked in different ways with audiences – requesting participation, picking out individuals, involving everyone as part of the piece – I now work in a formal audience/performer manner, but organise discussions after the performances. I do not want to challenge the audience as an 'audience' – a body of people who are there live – but want to be involved in an immediate process of questioning ideas and beliefs through live art and conversation with people who come and see my work.

I 'survive' (after a fashion) as an arts administrator and coordinator of Feminist Arts News (FAN) magazine, and am involved with a group of women cultural practitioners from Leeds and Bradford. We came together from a need to encourage and reassure our individual activities. So often women think of loads of reasons why not to do a piece of work – needs more research, no time, no energy, no money, not thought out enough, must do the washing, clean the windows...when others (!) just get on with it. So that is what we do now – get on with it!

Photo: Sue Ball, Photo Plus

7 • Creating performances

by Anne Seagrave

The majority of people who create works of art do so independently and unfunded, with the tenacious belief that at some point in the future someone may appreciate their endeavour enough to buy, fund or pay for it. Until this time, work may be restricted by lack of funds but it is well worth noting the undeniable value of being free from the constraints and manipulations of funding structures.

Working independently allows for the necessary 'time' to be sensitive to your own capabilities and limitations and to provoke changes in these as the work develops. During this time, a fine sense of your aims will naturally formulate, producing stronger, clearer work.

On the whole, venues are receptive to performance and one event may give rise to many others. Initially though, you will need to create your own opportunities in order for the work to be seen. Developing your own work, through presentations you have organised yourself (eg room above a pub/art college space/street venue) is an ideal opportunity.

Most of all, the creation of an informal environment with a sympathetic atmosphere and licence to experiment is invaluable. Having had the opportunity to present work, be receptive to criticism and learn from your mistakes, as this rapidly improves the quality of content and presentation.

Working on your own

It is an advantage to be versatile, devising performances initially which are adaptable to different spaces. As a result, you will have more opportunities to present your work. It is extremely beneficial to see as much 'live' performance as possible, whether it is music, poetry, theatre, cabaret or dance. Watching other performers work is very informative. If anything, you will be left with vivid memories of several performance nightmares and a few truly outstanding works which may later influence your own. Do approach performers you appreciate, pick their brains for useful names and addresses of venues sympathetic to live art works. As a solo performer you maintain complete artistic control without compromise, allowing yourself the luxury of taking the necessary 'time' for a piece to develop. You are responsible only to yourself instead of a company of fellow performers, it gives you the freedom to pursue alternative ventures without jeopardising a company's future. By working alone, performance pieces can be produced on a relatively small budget. Good quality solo work may be doubly attractive to venue promoters as your fee will be less than that of a group. Small venues are perfect, and there are many of them. Making work which is portable, allowing easy use of public transport, is convenient, cheap and of enormous advantage. Finally, when presenting a live art work to the public, you can achieve the intimacy of a one-to-one relationship with the audience, commanding their attention entirely by your own actions and dialogue.

As a company

Working with a group of talented fellow artists can be extremely inspiring, allowing elaborate performance pieces to be produced within a relatively short space of time, as ideas are 'bounced off' the members of the company. Organisational tasks can be designated allowing more time to be spent on the collective creation of the work. Companies are more often eligible for funding. If successful, the stress of 'working on the cheap' can be relieved, albeit temporarily. Publicity and photographs can be ordered in larger quantities saving money in the long term. Many promoters are more receptive to companies, considering their work easier to 'sell' than one-person shows. Workshops are more fun and travelling to venues is less boring and safer than alone. Finally, company support when things go badly, professionally or personally, can be invaluable.

Because of its open frontiers and flexibility of approach, live art is arguably the most responsive art form to the complexity and intensity of ideas and images that confront us at the end of the twentieth century.

Lois Keidan, ACGB Live Art Strategy discussion paper, 1991

Presenting work in public

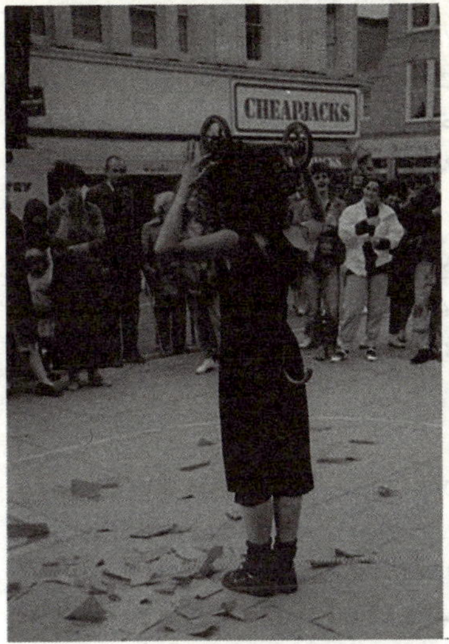

Anne Seagrave, **street performance, 1984. Performance defined by chalk circle on pavement.**

Consider basic practicalities affecting the audience's appreciation of your work such as: can they see the performance; can they hear the performance; are they going to be accidentally choked by smoke, soaked by water, etc.

Make a point of informing spectators if using such effects as strobe lighting, fire, smoke or excessive noise. Do this by simply showing courtesy and respect for your audience's interest. Think very carefully about the use of audience participation. Is this the strongest, most appropriate method, or could it be humiliating and weak? Do not think simplistically that the longer the performance, the more the audience will be interested. This is a major misconception.

Be sure to plan your own entrance and exit as clambering through a sea of spectators limits dramatic impact. It may be advisable to prepare yourself in case of uninvited interruptions (verbal or physical) from members of the audience. Finally, do not underestimate how genuinely interested and sympathetic an audience can be. If mishaps occur, deal with them professionally and as quickly as possible and the audience will almost certainly be supportive and maintain interest.

Street performances

Public parks and gardens, shopping centres, tents and marquees, derelict buildings, bridges, etc.

It's worth reminding yourself that what we're doing is strange, or at least unusual, in contemporary society. We put ourselves on the line, we may well be provoking the audience in different ways, which we may not even be aware of. So, it's not surprising if both we and the audience feel odd afterwards.
Richard Layzell

- Shouting to attract an audience's attention can be very tiring. Stillness, defining the space precisely, eg through a walking pattern/chalk circle on floor, or music may be more effective.
- If using voice, possibly choose an outdoor site which is sheltered from traffic noise or with good acoustics – a tunnel or pedestrian walkway, etc.
- Once you are considering a site, if possible visit it a number of occasions beforehand. (What is a quiet cul-de-sac on a Sunday may be Sainsburys back delivery entrance during the week.)

- The elements may be against you. If it is lashing rain or a thunderous gale, you are not any less a serious committed artist if you wait for the weather to improve or move to a sheltered site.
- It is a good idea to have a friend/minder with a camera close at hand to document your work and also deter members of the public from harassment or possible assault (which can happen).
- Respect the audience's right of way.

Gallery performances

see 9 • Touring performances

Public museums, private galleries, art school spaces, exhibitions, media shows, cultural centres, conferences, etc.

Find out in advance relevant information such as:

- Does the gallery have seating?
- Can a blackout be obtained?
- Is the gallery 'open plan' (eg with a café – this can be noisy)?
- Will there be a current exhibition on the days you are to perform, which may be distracting for you or your audience?
- What is the floor covering? Carpet which could hinder a movement performance, stone which could be uncomfortable or cold, or a surface that is uneven or slippery.
- Is there other lighting available in addition to the gallery lights?
- Will a gallery representative introduce your piece or, if it is a durational work, will there be a representative there as minder?
- Is there a room available for dressing/preparing for the performance?
- Is the gallery at ground level with floor length windows (the reaction of passers-by to the performance may be distracting to you or the audience or it could be exploited as an aspect of the work).

Theatre performances

Cinemas, studio theatres, dance venues, poetry rooms, proscenium arch stages, etc. Find out:

- What is the seating capacity and is it raked or flat?
- Is the stage raised or floor level?
- Are the audience on three sides, facing or surrounding the performance area (in the round)?
- Will there be someone to introduce your performance if required?
- Do you need your own technician? If so, can the same technician work both lighting and sound requirements?

- What is the background to the performance space – black or white, brick or cloth, etc.
- If members of the audience wish to leave during the performance, do they have to cross the stage space in order to do so?
- Is the sound desk beside the stage area or in a technical box? (If beside the stage, the 'click' of stopping and starting of cassette tapes can sometimes be distracting to performer and spectators).
- Are latecomers to be admitted? Are children to be admitted? As the performer you have a say on these decisions.

Pub/club performances

Discos, function rooms, bars, community halls, music venues, night clubs, cabarets, etc.

Many are divided into mixed billings, with more than one performance event on each night. Meet with the venue organiser and other 'acts' earlier to decide the best running order. If you are on after other acts ask:

- Are they using anything which may make the flooring slippery, sticky or wet, etc?
- How long will it take for them to clear the space once they have finished?
- Are they using smoke, fire, stink bombs or anything which could empty the venue of spectators before you come on?
- What is the duration of the piece before you?

Enquire as to whether the bar is in the same room as the stage area. This can be very distracting, with members of the audience shouting drink orders and tills ringing. Ask the venue to close the bar during your piece, perhaps providing an interval if the piece is over thirty minutes long. Most venues are accommodating.

Ask what technical equipment is available. A pub or club venue usually has limited equipment and may not have a resident technician. If possible visit the venue beforehand, asking:

- Are the audience all seated? In pubs and clubs there is often standing room for twenty at the very back, which can be hot and uncomfortable for those standing and noisy and distracting for yourself and the seated spectators.
- Whether the audience are on three sides, facing or surrounding the stage area and note also the background to the stage space, ie flock wallpaper, the toilets, etc.

An inexperienced organiser may think that by putting you on last, you are 'topping the bill'. You may therefore find yourself performing at 1am after the band, raffle and disco. If you are not happy with this, speak out.

Working as economically as possible

see 13 • Documentation

Venues usually require 8" x 10" black and white photographs for their publicity. Do not send out photographs of your work unless you are specifically requested as they are seldom returned, and this can be very expensive. Present the organiser with an alternative, ie drawing, collage, montage, etc. which will be cheaper and most likely more effective. Try not to be intimidated by glossy high cost publicity of other artists and companies. Spend time instead. If a venue asks for 100 posters and 1000 handbills and this is financially unacceptable for you, try to reach a compromise – you give them an image for their own 'what's on' leaflet and offer to make a visual display for their front of house, with photographs/collage and information on your work, which could be returned to you afterwards. Find out well in advance, whether your payment is to be a 'door split', (box office 30% and you keeping 70%) or is it to be a guaranteed fee. And always ask *how and when* you are to be paid? This could be in order of most appropriate methods, taking say:

- Cash on the night
- Cheque on the night
- Cheque to be posted
- Post-dated cheque (yes this does happen)
- You invoice the organisation and they apply for your fee from the relevant county council/funding body.

Even if you are presenting a free performance, always ask for expenses.

Finally

A cool head and a diplomatic approach is always an asset. This could try the patience of a saint and may not be in your nature but it really does help to maintain a professional, constructive approach when dealing with promoters, technicians, administrators and fellow performers. Take an interest in reviews in magazines and newspapers, and possibly invite

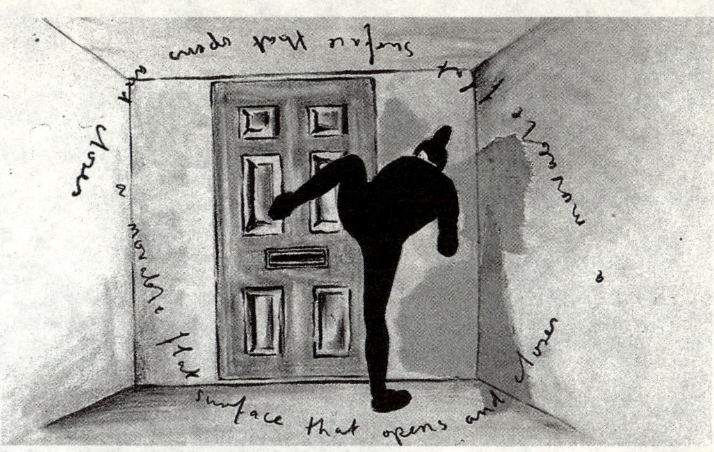

Or even what leaving was, **Anne Seagrave, 1990. Anne Seagrave often uses drawings like this for publicity as they are much cheaper to produce then photographs.**

a reviewer to attend one of your own pieces, once the opportunity to present a work has been secured. Finally and above all, do not underestimate the endless list of things that could go wrong while organising, travelling to and presenting live art works. Try to be as self-contained as possible, personally clarifying all details and arrangements in advance and if possible, taking any technical equipment you require with you.

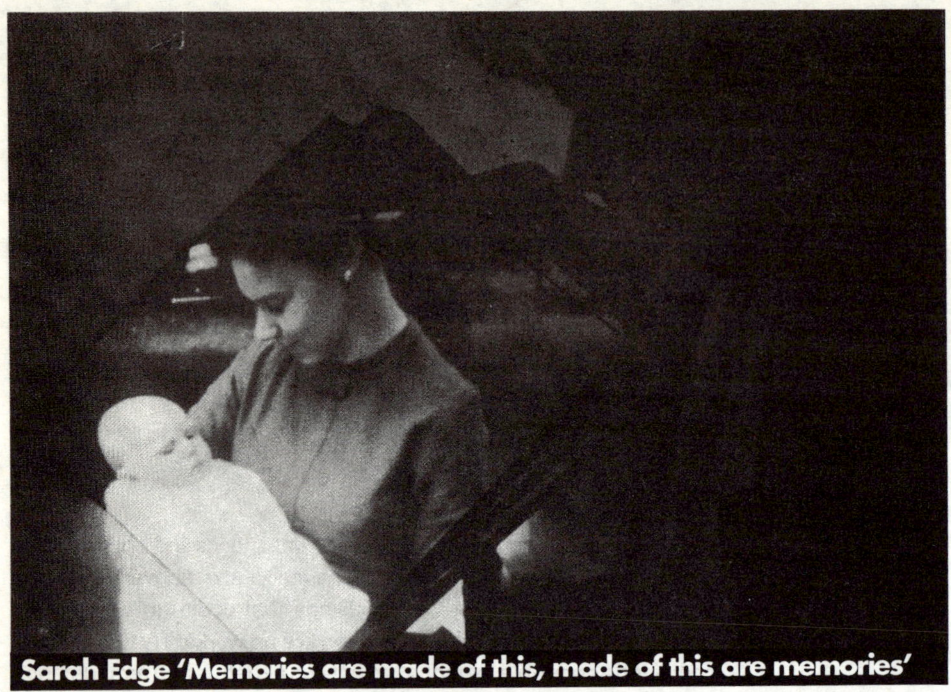

Sarah Edge 'Memories are made of this, made of this are memories'

I started working in live art at art college in Portsmouth, 1981. It was an easy move as prior to it I had been working with film and animation. My live work, like film, often has a narrative to it. Live art is my medium mostly because I feel more in control of it. Through the use of its different elements; image, sound and movement, and the comparison, conjunctions and dislocations you can cause by manipulating these elements I feel I can achieve a greater control over the type of messages I wish to put across in the work.

The audience for live art is variable and often determined by the spaces you choose to show in. My work is often made with a specific audience in mind. For example the performance 'The Essential Woman?' focuses on my experiences and unhappiness with the women's peace movement at the time. The work attempted to question notions of non-violence and essential female qualities. Its intended audience was women who were involved within the peace movement. I performed it at the National Greenham Common Conference in Manchester. I often perform at conferences, festivals, etc. Some work is intentionally made for these audiences. A work questioning the innocence of history is as relevant to history students, art historians or people interested in history as it is to people involved in the arts.

Surviving the event of performing means realising that you are the person in control. If things go wrong just carry on as best you can, your audience will follow how you determine the work to go.

8 • Preparing for a performance

by Mark Whitelaw of the Glee Club Performance Co

It is difficult writing about preparing for a performance without sounding like Akela reminding the cubs about what to pack for summer camp, and that in many respects is what it is like – travelling as lightly as possible, whilst covering any eventuality.

Ideally one begins performance preparations at the same time one begins work on the piece, prior to selling it to the promoter(s). At this stage considerations are broad: making a piece adaptable to fit into a number of venues if it is to tour, or using the full potential of a site if it is for a specific space. Work not built on site should be made to fit into whatever vehicle has been budgeted for, so find out both door size and capacity of a van before building it.

It is also very useful at this stage to draw up a checklist and diary. This should work backwards from the week when the creating of the piece begins, down to week one, the date of the performance. Put onto this all relevant deadline dates, ie when you expect/need to have certain things ready. The value of this is twofold, firstly it gives an idea of the amount of work needed at any given time and can be used in advance to make sure no fortnight is too heavy with unendurable tasks. Secondly, it is generally easier to work to a deadline, and self-imposed deadlines give a little more leeway. Once your checklist has been drawn up it is probably a good idea to display it where others can see it. You can be brought to boot publicly for not doing something – we generally are for our inability to get press and publicity photos together in good time.

Before the checklist can be properly filled out, there should be some discussion with the promoter(s) since their idea of deadlines can often differ wildly from yours. This is especially the case with venues which promote a good deal of work and produce programmes for a season, it is rare but these may need copy and photographs four or five months in advance. It is a good idea to get the names of the publicity officer and the technician if they exist. Many venues at this early stage will send you a pack containing contract, plan of space, list of deadlines

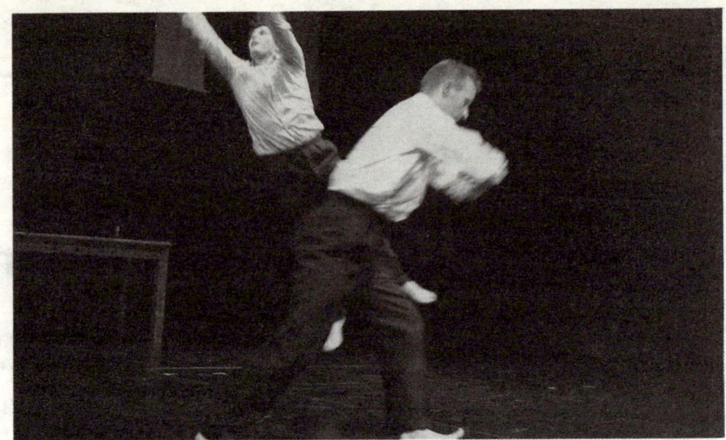

The Truth about the Russian Dancers, 1991, The Glee Club

and publicity requirements. Promoters that do not have regular performances may not do this as a matter of course, so it is a good idea to make sure they provide you with it as soon as possible. With this information you will be able to complete/amend your checklist and see how realistic it is.

During this time you will need to contact the promoter only occasionally, although it may be more often if the promoter doesn't normally promote work, or if you have a special relationship with them (eg your piece is being built especially for their space). Most venues tend to have their own daily routines, with some staff working office hours while others work a much later day, this should be borne in mind whenever you are contacting the venue – technicians tend not to be in at 9am and can be difficult to get hold of. It is important you talk to the technician before your performance as the printed material they provide on equipment, etc isn't always completely accurate. In general, venues have quite good large scale equipment, but may fall down on smaller things like hammers and saws, you may need to find this out from the technician. Other pertinent questions to ask technicians involve things like:

- Which doors are fire doors, and so cannot be blocked?
- Are the signs for the fire doors in awkward or obtrusive places?
- Where close to the venue can you buy materials that you may need? (It is strange how difficult it is to get fishing wire in some cities).

Try to reassure the technician that working with you on the day will be the best, easiest, most exciting, relaxing time s/he has had all month.

Technicians are the people you'll spend most time with and be most reliant upon, so it is especially important you don't upset them. The first rule is to arrive on time – we arrived 45 minutes later than we said we would for our last performance, to find six technicians/stage managers waiting for us and were glared at by a group of eyes that outnumbered ours 2:1. It is important to try to plan a realistic arrival time. Include time for things to go wrong and time to prepare yourself mentally for the performance, as well as the actual time it takes to get the performance ready. When you arrive and know what you want, explain this as clearly as you can to the technician. Most technicians may have to go off to do other things during the day, so it is best to know when they are going to be with you, and organise your day around that.

Venues, and to a lesser extent events, tend to have their own audiences, in terms of age, income bracket, etc. You can sometimes gauge the type of audience you will get by the layout style and hidden attitudes of the venue, particularly the bar or café if the venue has one. By knowing the kind of people that use the space for other things, or knowing the type of audience the promoter normally attracts, and the kind of audience you'll get, all might indicate how the performance will be received.

When the performance is seen, something will inevitably not go as planned, something always goes slightly adrift. Generally, where possible, it is better to ignore these and to carry on, or to change tack slightly to accommodate the problem. The chances are you will be the only person who notices. Some problems are too obvious and it's better to point it out, either by your actions or by telling the audience exactly what has happened – after all they are your rules to break. The worst thing you can do is to pretend something isn't happening when everybody watching knows that it is.

Every time I perform I'm frightened to death. Afterwards I maintain an initial high, then get terribly depressed. It's exhausting mentally, and my own assimilation of the work only connects months later, sometimes with small things that make me realise I've pin-pointed something.
Andre Stitt

Once your performance is over you have the sometimes odious task of trying to assess it. If your opinion and an objective audience's are the same, then it is relatively easy. Difficulties begin when they differ. The biggest problem we find, is not when the audience doesn't like it – there can be a million valid reasons why this is, and you can either take the criticisms on board or decide to ignore them. For us the big problems come when we don't like it but the audience does. The difficulty here is in knowing whether to trust your original idea of what the piece should be, or let it develop into something else, and this can be a very difficult decision to make. It can be just as difficult as trying to identify whether problems are innate to the piece (built into the structure) or are specific to the performance of it (not built into the structure) and, although this distinction cannot and should not be drawn always, a notion of it should be present in the assessment of your piece.

Sometimes it all goes completely wrong, and the thing fails on every level. Although 'pick yourself up, dust yourself down' is the kind of thing people get shot for saying, it's still more or less apt. Rarely if ever when things go so wrong, is it the result of one thing. It is usually a combination of things, some of which you couldn't have foreseen, from how the piece was marketed (and therefore the audience's expectations), to you being the fiftieth performance that week to use three bags of peat and Yugoslavian national dress.

Pre-performance preparations, whether long or short term, are about travelling light but having all eventualities covered. This may mean being more flexible about how your piece is seen, but this flexibility brings its own rewards. Finally, the only thing I remember Akela telling me as a cub packing my rucksack, was always carry a plastic bag with you: they take up very little room, and are very useful, not only for carrying things, but also for separating your wet clothes from your dry ones.

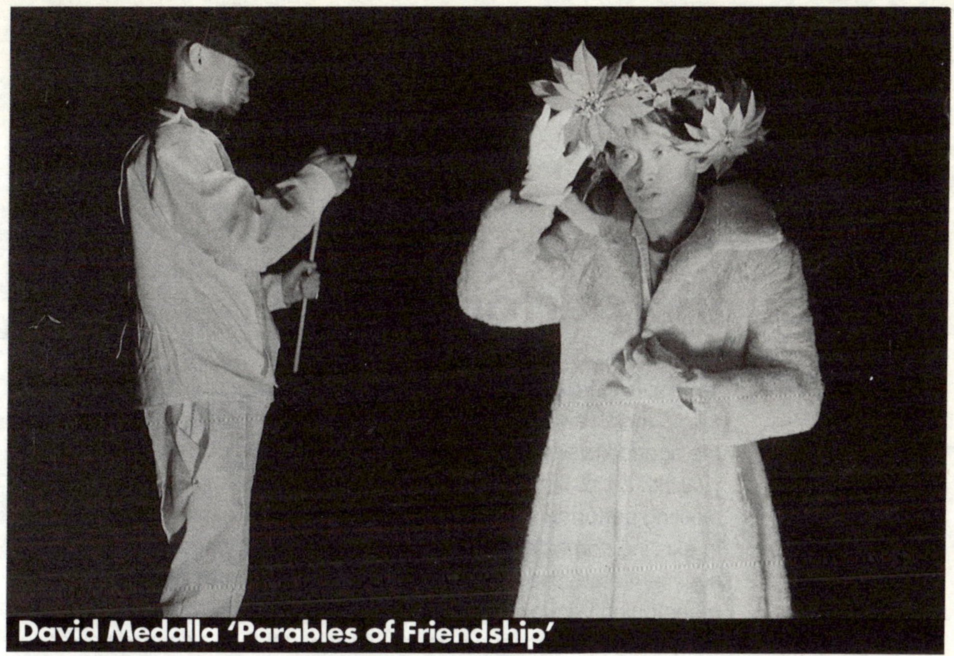

David Medalla 'Parables of Friendship'

Live art is direct, spontaneous and ephemeral. I started to work in it to find ways of integrating the various art forms I practise – painting, poetry, dance, music and film. In 1954, while living in New York, I started to invite friends to my apartment to live events (happenings) I devised and enacted. I respond to a variety of audiences and working situations often inviting the audience to participate in my event. I believe in adapting my art to all sorts of circumstances. Often, when travelling, in order to survive, and get to know people in a 'foreign' place, I approach nightclub managers and the like to allow me to give performances.

Part of the fun of giving a live performance is the possibility of things going wrong, especially if one is using technological devices. Adrenalin starts flowing when the audience responds during the course of a performance. Even a 'hostile' audience can be activated positively by a performer, as long as the performer is concentrated in putting across his/her ideas, vision, feelings, with imagination and an instinctive way of improvising to all manners of unforeseen situations and events. The important thing, for me, is not to insult the audience, whoever that audience may be, sympathetic or not to the performance artist. In performing I carry a dialogue with the audience (verbal, visual, musical, in terms of movements and images), and I extend this dialogue into the individual memories of every member of the audience.

The photo shows David Medalla (on right), with a member of the Baroque Buddha Brotherhood, performing 'Parables of Friendship' at midnight 24 June 1984, as the finale of the Second International Festival of Performance Art.

9 • Touring performances

by Mark Waddell

Touring live art in this country is difficult. It must be carefully planned and the financial rewards are often minimal. Currently, the power is held and the agenda is set by promoters and funding bodies, not the artists. It is vital that artists be pro-active as well as re-active, and not only follow the existing performance circuit but also attempt to initiate their own either in existing contexts, totally unused spaces or in unusual arts contexts such as literature festivals. Artists should not underestimate the value of researching venues/festivals and careful targeting and should not shy away from initiating ideas. Artists often forget they also hold power, for without them there would be no art and no venues and no jobs for those in the arts institutions. The mere realisation that power does also rest in their hands will help artists to be strong when confronted with the bureaucracy of established venues and circuits.

The basis of live art is experimentation and by its very nature there will be successes and failures. But this is not always acknowledged by promoters and funding bodies so it is essential to be confident in the work one tours. It must be of a professional standard, second chances are few and far between.

Why tour?

Live art has recently enjoyed an upsurge in interest. Events such as the National Review of Live Art and the Edge festivals are indicators of this. But audiences are still very specialist – mainly artists, practitioners, administrators and promoters. Reasons for touring are to develop:

see • 11 Live art promoters

- Interest in the medium from the general public
- Work in front of live audiences
- A national reputation which will put the artists in a stronger position to obtain more bookings, funding and media coverage

- The long term goal for the artist to be able to survive financially through the art form (given the current arts climate this is optimistic).

There are also reasons against touring:

- It is financially restrictive as costs are high and fees low.
- One can sometimes feel unwelcome, arriving at a venue to find no-one there to meet you – little support and small audiences.
- It can be exhausting.

What is tourable work?

The work one tours must:

- Be able to physically fit into the spaces you are targeting
- Be able to work technically in the venue, ie your lighting and sound should be 'feasible' and 'realistic'
- Be able to set up in the space within a reasonable amount of time. (Usually venues only offer the space for the day of performance. One should never under-estimate the time needed to install a set/environment, set up and focus the lights and complete a technical run-through of the performance. A technical run-through involves the artist walking through the piece with lighting and sound so the resident technician can note down the cues. This should be completed at least one hour prior to the performance).
- Be financially viable, ie the money obtained from the venue should at least cover your costs.

see 'The practicalities of touring' below

How to obtain bookings

Firstly, a decision must be made regarding who will administrate and organise the tour. It is essential that there is only one person liaising with the relevant venue to avoid confusion. Ideally one should have an experienced administrator who understands and is committed to the work.

Most venues do not book work cold – that is, very few are booked because of mailing out information packs and publicity (instead these act as a back-up). Most venues tend to book work they have seen live and liked and can afford. Sometimes performances are booked on the strength of a video and/or press reviews. If the artist is unknown

A belief in the value of your own work and ideas is the most important thing.
Claire Spafford: Glory what Glory

it is sensible to use whatever financial resources to make a video on VHS and to print good quality professional publicity material. It is best to provide promoters with a full length video of the performance so they can get a feel for the shape of the work. However, the best way to obtain bookings is to get promoters to see the work live. Unfortunately, this is not easy as promoters are not usually very good at attending showcases of unknown work.

If you have the time and money it is worth considering hiring an established space and inviting promoters and funders to the event. The ICA hires out the theatre for such events. If a promoter sees your work and is supportive, ask him/her to act as a referee – ideally you should ask him/her to write a letter about your work recommending you for bookings. This could be photocopied and sent to venues.

Research potential venues by talking to venues, regional arts boards, arts councils, promoters and other artists. Do not limit your research to this country. Mainland Europe offers more opportunities and higher financial rewards. It is necessary to find out the following information:

- Contact name of programmer
- The venue's policy
- Technical facilities and size of space
- Average audience attendance
- If they promote work outside of the building
- How often they produce publicity brochures – ask them to send you one
- What sort of publicity/press back up they provide the artist
- If they encourage and can organise educational activities linked with the performance, eg workshops.

Approach

Once you have researched the venues and found which might potentially be interested in the work and can accommodate it technically you should send the venue a typed letter outlining:

- Work
- Educational activities if relevant
- Performance fee (put 'negotiable' in brackets)
- When you are looking to tour.

If possible you should include some publicity material, press reviews/ previews and an information pack which could cover in more detail:

- The work/company
- Biographies
- Performance history
- Referees
- Technical requirements
- Press reviews.

However, more important than an information pack is a good quality promotional video. In your letter ask whether the programmer would like to see the video. If so, send it. The letter should be pro-active and professional and explain that you will (if possible) provide the venue with publicity within their required deadlines, know their artistic policies and audience and will work hard to ensure that the event is a success. Make the venue feel confident that you will provide a successful performance of a professional standard and show you know the venue and have done research. Follow this up with a phone call a week later.

Once initial contact has been made with a venue, regular telephone conversations follow and notes are kept about each venue's response ('likely', 'unlikely', 'possible', 'no way!' etc, etc). We have also found supplying a couple of respected promoters' names as referees can prove useful.
Claire Spafford: Glory what Glory

Finance

Once you have interested the venue in your work and they have agreed in principle to booking you, it is time to talk money. Firstly you must work out your costs per performance so that you know the minimum financial deal you can accept.

Sample budget

Expenditure	5 performers @ £50 each	£250.00
	1 hired van	£70.00
	Food, 5 people @ £10 each	£50.00
	Petrol	£20.00
	Hire of specialist technical equipment	£30.00
	Accommodation: 5 people @ £15 each	£75.00
	Total expenditure	£495.00
Income	Minimum to break even fee	£495.00
	Total income	£495.00

The above shows that you cannot accept a fee of less than £495.00 for one performance without making a loss or not paying yourselves. However, if you are provided with accommodation, transport, food, etc then the minimum fee can be reduced. This fee obviously only covers the performance. It provides no income to devise future performances, research venues, do publicity, etc. The ability to negotiate fees is important.

A wide range of financial deals will be offered to you including a box-office split (percentage of the door takings, usually offered at a 70:30 split in favour of the artist). It is only worth considering such an offer if:

- You wish to perform at the venue/festival and are prepared to make a loss.
- The venue has good audiences and you feel confident the door money will cover your costs.

If you are offered a box-office deal ask the venue whether they will provide a guarantee – for example of £100 so that should no-one turn up you at least have some income. The most favourable deal is a set performance fee which covers your costs.

Contract

see 16 • Contracts

Once you have agreed a financial deal and date, the venue will send you a contract which you must read carefully, amend if necessary and return within the agreed deadline. Make sure you agree all details such as time of arrival, technical support, press and publicity support, travel, food and accommodation as this should be included in the contract.

Providing information

The next step is to provide the venue with all the necessary information for the best promotion, presentation and appreciation of the work. If you are performing at a venue for a reasonable run you may feel it is worthwhile printing some special publicity, this should be discussed with the venue as they may agree to help out with the costs and at the very least they should distribute it for you. Venues may expect to see copy for their approval before you print. Put together a mailing list of your contacts, friends, anyone who you think will be interested in the performance and ask if the venue can mail it for you and use it to promote the performance.

Never assume anything

Make sure you tell the venue if you do not have a technician or administrator to avoid confusion. Ask the venue to brief the box-office staff on the type of work that you will be presenting. Chase up venues and ensure your publicity has been distributed. Liaise with them about press, publicity and technical requirements and to make sure that you have the correct logos and copy. A good idea is to send four paragraphs to each venue which should be passed on to all the staff, especially the box-office staff explaining:

- Why you're coming to the venue
- The company and why its touring
- Target audiences
- Press and publicity suggestions.

I've had some very bad experiences, for all sorts of reasons, most frequently because I wasn't clear about the kind of venue or kind of larger event that it was part of.
Richard Layzell

The practicalities of touring

Touring can often be exhausting and frustrating which is why it is essential to prevent as many problems as possible from happening. One should liaise with the venue as much as possible about administrative details of print, press, box-office staff being briefed, technical details, time of arrival, etc. Ring the venue to ensure your publicity has been sent out at the agreed time, enquire about any press previews or reviews and to ask where your publicity has been sent. Try to ensure it provides you with the same technician for each performance.

Before setting off to the venue prepare a checklist:

- Date and time of arrival at venue
- Venue address and telephone number
- Name of administrative contact
- Name of technical contact
- Lighting plan and agreed technical arrangements
- Plan of space
- Time agreed in the performance space
- Starting time of the performance
- Free facilities offered by the venue
- Agreed cost of any facilities the venue may have hired into the space for your performance and when this must be covered
- Ensure that you have a copy of the contract
- If the venue is not providing food take your own as it will be cheaper
- Number of complimentary tickets you are allowed

- Programmes – if you have them
- Equipment list – hired, borrowed, where from and when it has to be returned
- If the venue has any of your videos, photographs, information packs – make sure they return them to you on the day of performance
- Any invoice to the venue if this has been agreed. If already invoiced and they have agreed to pay on the day, take a copy of the invoice with you.

Once at the venue – behave professionally so they will invite you back.

After the tour

After the tour there will be certain administrative details to be completed such as returning borrowed or hired equipment, invoicing the venue, chasing up payment and finding out feedback from the venue on your work. It is worth sending a questionnaire to each venue asking them to answer a few simple questions. You can keep this information for your own records and maybe also to show to funding bodies:

- Box office details – number of full price and concessionary tickets sold
- The performance – ie any feedback from audiences and venue
- Publicity – comments
- Press – please enclose any press previews/reviews and comment on press coverage
- Technical
- Administration
- Future projects – would you be interested in booking the company in the future?
- Audiences – do you feel this performance has helped develop interest in live art in the region?

After the venue has returned the questionnaire it is also worth sending them a short summary of your experiences at the venue, eg whether you were made to feel welcome, if your agreements such as technical assistance were kept to and any comments you feel important. These letters could also be sent to funding bodies after the tour to inform those in power of the way that artists are being treated at venues.

Summary

- Be confident in the work – don't put out sub-standard work
- Research venues – know who you are approaching and why
- Don't be afraid to initiate ideas
- Be professional in your approach with typed letters, good printed matter
- Once booked, give venues all the information they need for the best promotion, presentation and appreciation of the work
- Think Mainland Europe as well as this country
- Never assume anything – liaise with venues regularly
- Charge enough to cover costs
- Be strong – insist on respect
- Choose an administrator
- Research and target venues carefully
- Make a video
- Get a promoter to see work live and act as referee
- Only accept financial deals that you can afford
- Liaise with venues regularly
- Return contract
- Chase up payments
- Obtain feedback
- Send questionnaire to venues
- Send your comments to venues on how you were treated.

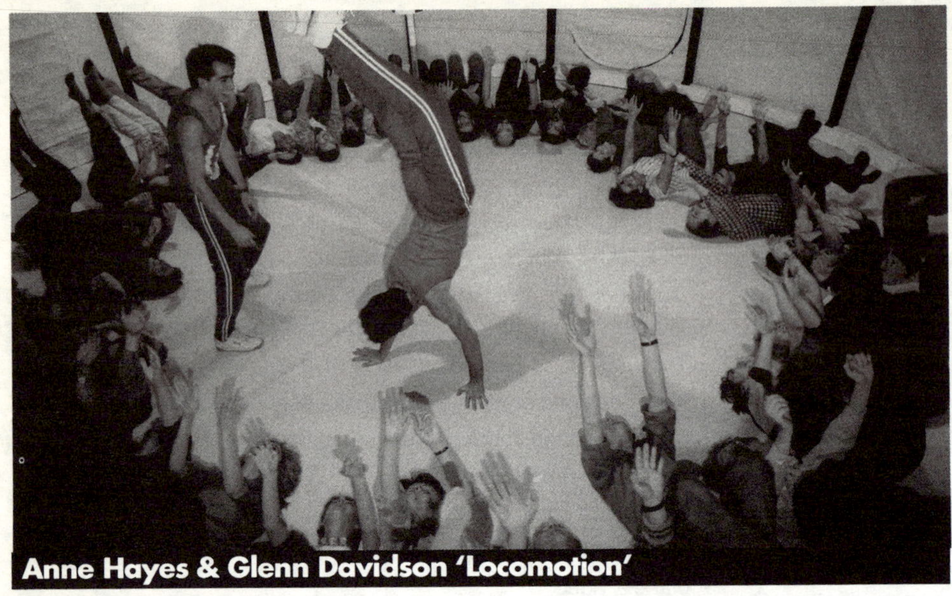

Anne Hayes & Glenn Davidson 'Locomotion'

The active participation of audience is a dominant feature of our work. 'Locomotion' is an example, where the performance was the three performers, the audience and the installation – an enclosed kinetic environment.

The exploratory beginnings of 'Locomotion' happened in the latter half of a year long live art residency at Llanover Hall Arts Centre Cardiff 1984. I think it was the open brief of the residency that allowed the evolvement of our work to include the audience – to squeeze the boundary between performance and the perceptual exploration possible in workshops.

Glenn and I collaborate regularly with Geoff Moore (Moving Being) in performances involving dancers, actors, etc. I find this of interest in relation to working alongside people who have performance techniques of a very different order. They have skills/disciplines/conventions I don't have as an artist performer.

Survival is very difficult in Wales – in 1980 no funding category existed. We managed to get an exhibition grant of £4500 to buy a vehicle and tour in Wales (akin to small theatre group) from the Welsh Arts Council and have had subsequent grants in the region of £2000 and £3000. For 'Locomotion' and workshops we charged fees between £1000 and £1200 per week. We have always done a lot of workshops and in the past year have done some part-time and visiting hours in various colleges.

We always find it better to be involved in publicity – venues can write highly inappropriate things – especially people who come from a theatre background. An infamous case was a venue who described us as using 'various props' – in a performance that involved the audience in a direct experience of their own perceptions.

10 • Approaching promoters

by Mike Stubbs

Is the most important aspect of promoting yourself as an artist to make what you yourself consider to be good art? If you don't believe in what you are doing why should anyone else? Likewise you know yourself when you are acting in bad faith or pandering to someone else's criteria, you might become a 'successful' artist but will you still have your own integrity to wrestle with? Most artists, promoters, interviewers, commissioners of any experience will see through the bullshit, but some will not. Do you want a 'career' as an artist? Many artists don't want arts organisations, projects, funding applications and schemes in their lives.

If you want to engage in a particular kind of artworld, you need to make your art and yourself known to those people and that world. Find the right kind of network. Getting information to the right people can rely on getting information yourself. Information gathering means looking at books like this but also talking to your mates, attending other artists' performances and keeping an address book of contacts.

The people who need most to see your work often seem to be those who mirror any insecurities you may have or who you distrust most – people with power and control; those who have the spending power or performance space. After sitting on my first Arts Council selection panel I was pleasantly surprised to find my assumptions of nepotism and corruption negated. There were panels of artists and organisers, many still struggling to find funds for their own work, some signing on. But the art world is small and inevitably, as in all areas of life, some level of 'in the know-ness' exists, yet its manifestation is a good pointer of how to promote yourself. Information travels fast. If I see someone with a good haircut, I might ask *'where did you get your haircut?'* If a well received performance has taken place in Glasgow it won't take long for other artists and promoters to find out in Hull or Sheffield.

Identify to whom you are promoting; why and what you want. Prioritise organisations and individuals you respect and feel may respect you. Avoid getting into the habit of expecting failure – it will affect the tone of your phone calls, letters and meetings. Many artists after years of 'loss making' have been unlucky, made bad art, have been victims of prejudice or have made art that is not fashionable or thought not 'important'. Identifying cultural norms, trends and historical prejudices is useful whether you wish to confront them or pander to other people's expectations.

This means having some understanding of who or what you are communicating with. Don't be afraid to ask for a commissioning or equal opportunities policy. Hull Time Based Arts like most organisations has a constitution, selection procedure, commissioning and equal opportunities policy. In devising projects it is a mixture of implementation of that policy and chance: fulfilment of policy as decided by the membership or management committee in relation to available space, sites or interesting concepts.

Imagine how you would like proposals and documentation presented if you had to look at them. An organisation such as HTBA may have to represent an artist or project to a potential venue or funding body. This means we need to understand the proposed project thoroughly and need supporting material to capture the imagination of someone else; possibly a potential sponsor, a regional arts officer who may be able to help or a health and safety inspector who might want to stop your project. A good way of doing this is to capture their imagination and work out ways of holding their attention not just through frequency, forcefulness and gimmickry, but with what really counts: developing ideas and presenting them clearly. This of course should be the same for how you present ideas to organisations in the first place. Be concise.

Documentation of previous, developing or proposed work consisting of slide pack, video, CV, reviews, written description is essential, especially when sending it to someone who does not know you or your work. Making a lot of slide packs or publicity packages can be cost effective and energy saving if you can afford it. If you want stuff back, state it clearly and to make it quicker send an SAE. Of course you never do get all your material back and nothing is worse than having to remind an organisation (who may possibly have rejected your proposal) to return a video or slides. But hairdressers and mechanics expect to make a 'loss' in their first years of trading. Should it be any different for artists? If affordable, VHS preview copies/documentation might be regarded as consumables. Unintentionally murky, grainy or out of focus videos are very likely to get fast-forwarded.

In terms of marketing/ publicising my work I have found that expensive presentation has become more and more important to grab people's attention – people want a strong image, good reviews and even better still, personal recommendations from promoters and critics.
Françoise Sergy

Drawings need to be clear whether impressionistic or technical. Detailed lists of spatial, technical and special requirements are very useful – if you are not yet sure of what you need, say so and ask for consultation during development. Similarly if you don't know how to schedule and cost a project realistically, ask for advice. A proposal for performance work 'in the community' should either state clearly which community, whether you already know them, age group, size, or it should indicate that you wish to undertake research, liaise with groups prior to arrival, why they should be interested and how you will do all this. If applying for a residency in a psychiatric hospital, make it quite clear, perhaps in a covering letter how you would cope in the situation, previous experience and a reference. Very rarely would an unknown artist be unleashed into a potentially difficult situation; for the protection of the residents of the hospital and the artist. For such a project we would interview the potential artist. At that interview we would hope to see someone who can mix with others. This might not be the case for another project where the artist wanted to bury themselves in a pit full of jelly.

Things to consider in making a proposal (many points fit happily under either heading):

What are you offering

- The idea
- The manifestation
- Previous work
- Documentation
- Involvement with other people
- Originality
- Has it been shown before
- Problems, dangers, difficulties.

What do you want

- Money
- Accurate costings
- Does it need space – what kind?
- Assistance/volunteers
- Technical requirements
- Publicity
- Preparation time
- Distribution.

Finally you may decide it is all a bit unpleasant, too competitive, that the potential for failure is too worrying and perhaps you would be better off staying well clear of the whole thing. Sometimes I feel like that.

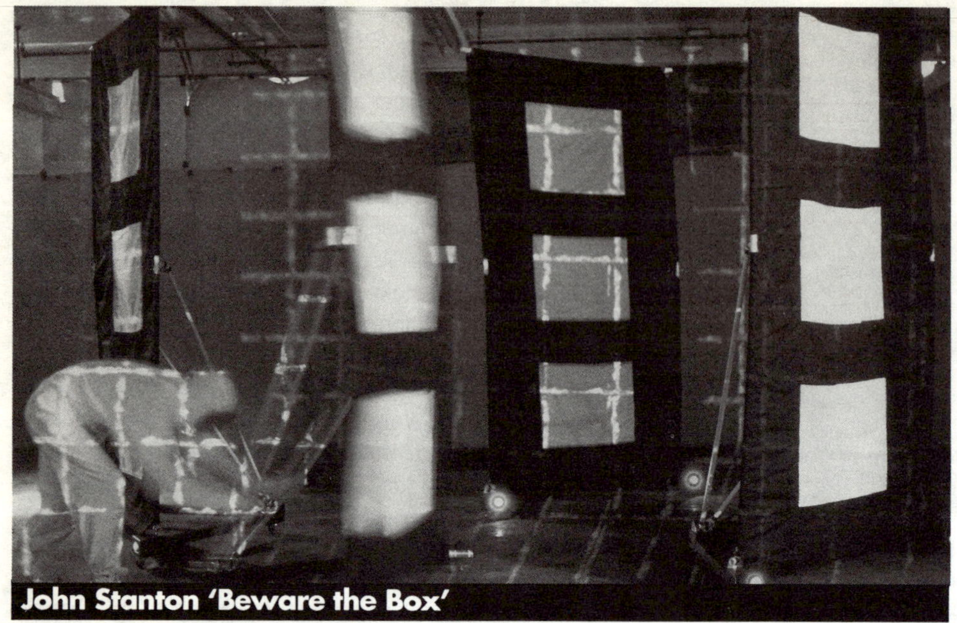

John Stanton 'Beware the Box'

In some ways it was largely by accident that I started to work in the area of live art. During my last term at college (Cardiff 1986) I had been making installations. For my final piece of work for my degree show I was unable to find a technical solution for moving certain objects around in an installation; the only solution was myself; so it stemmed from there. My work has continued more or less in this vein but I do not 'perform' as such – I am part of a time-based installation. It is because my work is installation based that I encounter huge problems when performing; partly because I am not that mobile!

It would also seem that there are almost two channels of funding oneself, both of which I have difficulty fitting into.

The first is what I call 'the club circuit' – ie venues like the Leadmill where you might be invited to perform as part of a 'package' of entertainment. It takes me a certain amount of time to load up my 'gear', normally having to hire a van then travel, unload, perform, and then home again, normally on the same night. For a fee of around or under £100, profit is slim and effort lots!

The second is installation commissions. For example TSWA, or similar. The prospect of doing installation work is far more attractive and far better paid. However as a 'young' still relatively unknown artist to compete against older, better known artists is continually depressing and predictable. You normally know who's going to get the grant or commission even before it's advertised. It's an uphill struggle.

11 • Live art promoters

by Anna Douglas

Over the years there has been a steady growth in the sheer number of organisations and individuals who are working in live art. In 1991/92 a startling variety of promoters competed for funds available through the Arts Council's Live Art Promoters Scheme and their new scheme designed for interdisciplinary projects, the New Collaborations Fund, received an enormous number of applications. But despite this healthy increase in production, the status of live art is still one of uncertainty.

see 14 • Funding

Live art's status

Live art is a diverse artistic practice, operating across disciplines and in a variety of formal and informal spaces. This inevitably presents an intriguing series of problems for promoters and ones which inevitably rebound on artists. For an artist whose work does not conform to Eurocentric expectations of performance art, the situation is further exacerbated. Promoters must challenge cultural stereotypes of innovation to embrace work from a diversity of cultures.

see 3 • Personal histories

Distribution

Artists depend heavily upon promoters to programme and commission work. Surprisingly the balance of provision between London and the regions favours the latter.

Throughout the country there are building-based gallery or theatre/events programmers, but there are also a significant number of non-building-based organisations who prioritise live art exclusively or that incorporate it into other time-based or site-specific activities.

Frustratingly there is not a formal promoters network that artists can take advantage of; rather informal relationships between practitioners, producers and promoters. Too often an organisation programmes live

Decisions vital to our future in terms of funding and recognition are made totally undemocratically by a tiny proportion of individuals.... Which is why I feel it's so important for artists to set up our own projects and venues, so we can create more opportunities for ourselves and in the long run bypass the existing networks....
Françoise Sergy

art due to the determination and enthusiasm of a particular individual rather than expressed as programming policy: an organisation's enthusiasm for live art can easily evaporate if the enthusiast moves on.

The promoters

So, where do artists turn to show work and have it commissioned? The answer is as variable as live art itself. Indeed the plurality of the art form dictates a range of promoters.

Art galleries

Over the last few years an increasing number of art galleries have begun to present live art. With encouragement offered through the Arts Council's development schemes, many municipal galleries including the Laing in Newcastle, Manchester City Art Gallery, Cartwright Hall in Bradford, Stoke on Trent, Wolverhampton and Southampton Art Galleries have included live art in their contemporary art programmes. Presently the Arts Council is assisting the Ferens Gallery in Hull, The Garage Arts Space in Walsall and Cleveland Gallery to establish a network of purpose-built, high-quality live art spaces. Many independent galleries with experimental art programmes; Kettles Yard in Cambridge, Ikon in Birmingham, Museum of Modern Art in Oxford and others, understand live art's role in contemporary culture and regularly promote work.

Staging work in galleries can be rewarding, many have good educational departments and are developing new audiences, but presenting work in galleries can also be fraught. Due often to gallery or local authority bureaucracy, to public safety regulations, lack of facilities; dressing rooms, washing facilities, lighting, awkward performance spaces and unsuitable marketing, artists can all too often find their work unsympathetically managed. Quite simply, the easier work is to present, the less it 'disrupts' gallery spaces and the more it leans towards the visual arts rather than theatre or dance, the more enthusiastic a gallery is likely to be.

Multi arts centres

see 'Arts centres' 14 • Funding

Multi art centres are surprisingly not as sympathetic to live art as their name would suggest. Conflicts between studio theatres and gallery spaces as to who 'owns' live art, serve to emphasise the artform's dichotomy and British culture's 'territorialism'. Knowing which department to approach is a matter of trial and error. However Arnolfini in Bristol, the Third Eye Centre in Glasgow and the Cornerhouse in Manchester are examples of multi-media spaces that regularly support live art.

Studio theatres

Live art which is more theatrically based can adapt to fit the studio circuit that exists across the country. The Welsh, Scottish and Northern Ireland Arts Councils, and the English regional arts boards will have details of all the experimental, educational and studio theatres in their region. Whether or not a theatre programmer understands what an artist's work is about and is willing to physically accommodate it is, as is so often the case, dependent on their personal enthusiasm. But as a rule, studio theatres have the technical and promotional expertise most galleries do not possess.

see 20 • Contacts

Experimental venues

There is a handful of venues in Britain, the ICA in London, the Greenroom in Manchester, the Zap Club in Brighton and the Third Eye Centre in Glasgow who have pioneered the development of theatre based live art. At various times these venues stage platform events in collaboration with promoters throughout Britain to showcase emerging artists.

Festivals

Edge Biennale in Newcastle, Contemporary Archives in Nottingham and the National Review of Live Art at the Third Eye in Glasgow are the most established and successful festivals of live art bringing together national and international programmes of commissioned and presented work in studio, gallery and site specific locations. Festivals such as these provide a focus for the live art sector and are important meeting grounds for artists, critics and prospective programmers.

I have also attended festivals both as performer and audience. I believe that they offer opportunities for witnessing a great deal of work in a short time, and are fun.
a. x. fraser

Increasingly established festivals such as London International Festival of Theatre (LIFT), Edinburgh International Festival, Glasgow's Mayfest, Brighton Festival and Liverpool Festival of Comedy, are incorporating live art into their programmes. Whether such initiatives are the result of trying to find something 'novel' to 'pep up' more traditional based programmes, the trend has certainly opened new doors for live artists.

Live art's assimilation into other cultural events has been relatively easy. Music, mime, dance, street and cabaret festivals have increasingly brought in experimental work to add variety to programmes. The 'packaged' nature of festivals may not please purists, but as a means to attract new audiences they deserve attention.

Even if an artist does not stage work in a platform event, just being around can often be a good way to meet promoters and exchange information.

Autonomous organisations

For artists who do not wish to work in either galleries or theatres there are a small number of organisations who specialise in site-specific projects. Freed from bureaucracy, they have the curatorial flexibility to respond to artist's needs and requirements. Organisations such as Hull Time Based Arts, the Gulbenkian (large scale projects), Events Space in Glasgow, Projects UK in Newcastle and ArtAngel in London have in the past invited applications for commissions to develop large-scale works. But having been at the forefront of developing non-building based art, it is fair to say that even these organisations are now finding it difficult to provide the financial resources needed to produce large scale works and to take risks on new artists.

Public art agencies

Though traditionally commissioning permanent environmental, or architectural projects, an increasing number of public art agencies are collaborating with organisations on live art projects. Although it is unlikely that these organisations will regularly take on the role of commissioning site specific live art, it is hoped collaborations like that between the Public Art Agency in Birmingham, the Ikon Gallery and Birmingham City Council will encourage other agencies to think about the possibilities of commissioning temporary public live works.

Artist-run organisations

For many artists who have been dissatisfied with professional promoters and the concentration of funds into a handful of organisations, the solution has been to join forces with other artists to promote themselves. Such artist-led initiatives are increasingly viable due to the Live Arts Commission Scheme set up by the Arts Council in 1988. Having replaced the old Performance Art Promoters Scheme (1985-88), which tended to fund large, and some argue monopolising, live art organisations, this later source of funding aims to encourage all promoters, established or new, groups or individuals, to culturally diversify, take risks and encourage audience and artistic development.

Others

Because of live art's strength in tackling contemporary issues, many live art projects are originated by local authority workers, teachers, artists in the community, educational establishments and so on. Usually these groups collaborate with professional arts programmers to commission work or residencies for particular sites; hospitals, schools, factories, housing estates, for example and often around particular themes. For artists who wish to produce work within collective community contexts, such promoters may offer the opportunity to work closely with facilitators and audiences.

How to approach a promoter?

see • 10 Approaching promoters

Who an artist will approach depends upon what area of live art activity they work in. Whilst there are no strict rules, promoters do have their preferred areas of interest: dance based, visual theatre, visual art based, site specific, installation, etc, and it is well worth taking the time to get to know them. Mailing lists are a crucial way of keeping in touch with promoter's ideas and plans, and artists should make sure that they regularly receive an organisation's promotional literature. Promoters are listed in the contracts section of this book and lists are available from the Arts Council.

Once an artist has defined which promoter specialises or might be interested in their line of work, they should begin to market it directly. Most programmers welcome CVs and promotional packs as it helps them build up a catalogue of artists for future reference.

A number of artists have chosen to hand the business of marketing their work over to promotional agents. Although in Britain this pioneering work is pursued only by a handful of professional individuals and the Arts Admin organisation in London, their role has been invaluable in championing the cause of live artists both at home and abroad, co-ordinating tours and securing media coverage.

Weaknesses

Because of their diverse nature, live art promoters do not all enjoy the same level of expertise, resources or skills in commissioning, staging and marketing live art. This can often result in frustration; poor facilities, undocumented, badly administrated projects, small audiences and most importantly impoverished artists. Only experience will reveal who is good at what.

Future developments

Future developments, initiated by the Arts Council and regional arts boards such as North West Arts, are encouraging potential promoters to programme experimental areas of work. By extending help with marketing and financially underwriting live art programmes, many regional venues are finally getting the support they need which can only mean good news for artists. For those artists who live in London, the future does not look so rosy. Until arts funding is sorted out in the capital promoters will continue to struggle to operate at all.

Except in extraordinary circumstances, live artists are dependent on promoters. Promoters are their... work and their spectators. The relationship is crucial, but, because of the variables in live art practice, there cannot be a proven way of getting it right.
Lois Keidan, ACGB Live Art Strategy discussion paper, 1991

The arrival of the single market in 1993 is a welcome opportunity for promoters to get British artists seen abroad, but touring work is, for many increasingly under-resourced organisations, not a prospect they relish. As in previous years it will be artists who will have to arrange their own international schedules rather than being able to rely on British promoters to advance their work on their behalf.

Ironically just at a time when live art's status seems to be on the increase, funding cuts and reductions in resources are making its promotion as difficult as ever.

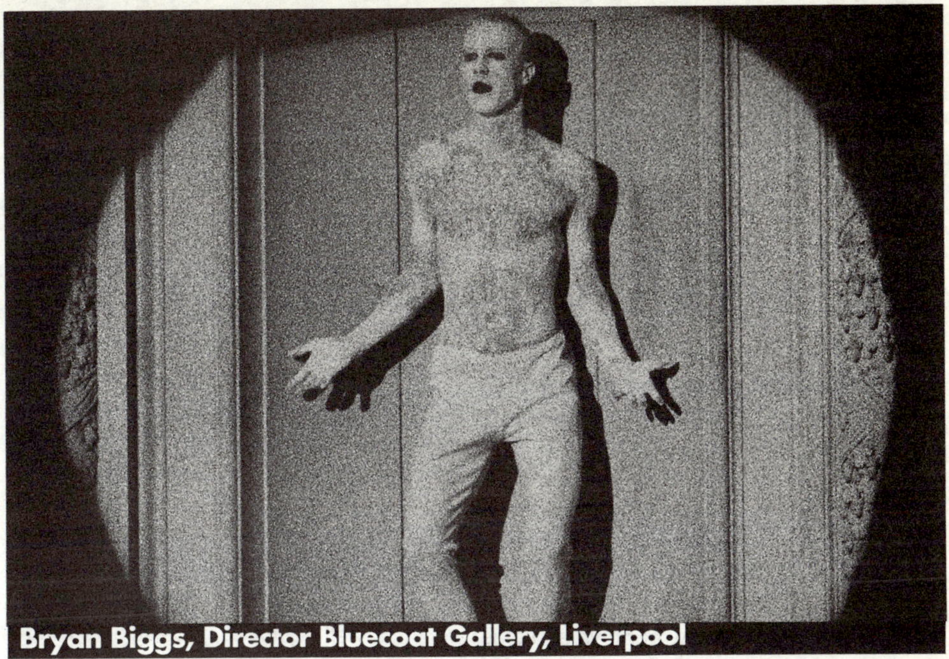

Bryan Biggs, Director Bluecoat Gallery, Liverpool

One problem for curators in promoting live work beyond the gallery is ensuring that the gallery, as promoters of the event, receives due credit for organising it. Handing out leaflets in the vicinity of the event is a good way of both helping to provide an understanding of the work and relating the piece back to the gallery if some accompanying exhibition/event is being staged there. This sometimes gives the performance the air of a political rally, but often is the only way of contextualising what might otherwise be an ephemeral, unrecorded event. Of course that may be the artist's intention, in which case keep a low profile!

It's never too soon to start planning. For highly public events always check competing events in the popular calendar well in advance. Liverpool group Visual Stress gave a large performance opposite Lime Street Station the night before the John Lennon memorial concert when 45,000 are expected to descend on the city.

The most successful events recently have been those challenging accepted definitions of live art (if such definitions exist), looking to live work outside a Western, art school tradition. 'Urban Vimbuza', by Visual Stress, was a refreshing, wholly local affair involving up to 100 performers, only about three of whom had an art school background. Bikers, African drummers and dancers, mountaineers, a rock band, a sound system and fashion models were brought together in a wild, at times chaotic evening performance. Pop Mechanica, from Leningrad, gave a similarly epic multi-media performance in collaboration with local people at St. George's Hall. The photo shows Robin Blackledge (who recieved the 1989/90 Bluecoat Award) performing at the event.
Photo: Will Curwen.

12 • Publicising performances

by Laurence Lane

The Quarter Club was set up in 1988 after a performance summer school at the Green Room. A number of new artists from different media but all with an interest in time-based work decided to form a transitory group for the creation and promotion of live art. We had regular meetings and, thanks to Stella Hall who was artistic director at the time, were given the use of all Green Room resources (photocopier, phone, stamps, envelopes, mailouts, etc) and the theatre space free of charge. As new, unsubsidised artists this gave us an unequalled opportunity to show our own and other work in a well-equipped, professional venue which was in itself a joy.

My work is difficult to 'sell' as it is short (half an hour) and limited audience. I am being forced by funding/ marketing pressure to create a longer piece and accomodate a larger audience.
Nenagh Watson

We started by putting on showcases of three or more artists/ groups. These were open to anyone who wanted to show their work. Since it was (and still is) often difficult to perform new work anywhere we didn't want to make any qualitative judgements. As long as the artists considered their work appropriate they could show it. We were, of course, restricted by the space and time scale of the showcases. I still think this was a very honourable idea but it meant that the quality of each event was unpredictable. On the marketing front we tried to make showcases an appealing selling point, promoting the whole event rather than individual artist.

Quarter Club showcases gained a reputation for showing 'interesting' work in an informal atmosphere, a little chaotic but not a bad night out. Our audience numbers ranged from 12 to 80, and out of the nine showcases we put on, three of them had a really good feel. The trouble was that apart from a hardcore handful there was no consistent audience, we didn't really know who we were appealing to. Every time we promoted we had no idea if anyone would come. We put on an event about every two months but we couldn't afford to keep the showcase running long enough for the audience we had attracted to build any

Always do your own publicity, and using 'hosts' publicity machine as a support to your own material. Marketing live art work is difficult when encompassing a relatively unknown audience.
Nenagh Watson

further. At this point we should have indulged in some basic market research.

Looking back, the actual promotion of the event was ridiculously low on our priority list. We used well designed if somewhat obscure posters, photocopied at first and then later very cheaply printed at a worker's co-operative. For distribution we relied on the Green Room's huge performance mailing list that seemed to go needlessly to the four corners of the earth, walking round Manchester putting posters up in prominent places, and the standard 50 words in the Green Room brochure.

Writing copy

The major contact between live art and the potential audience is made through posters, flyers and venue brochures. These are made up of various visual images and a few words of copy. Since the medium itself is about experimenting with everything, this paragraph is very important in trying to convey why the performance is worthy of attention. There is frequently no straightforward narrative and the exploration pursued is often philosophical and ethereal which means that such a limited means of expression might seem far from adequate. But, and I don't know how to say this without seeming arrogant, these 50 or so words often become more of an obstacle than an enlightenment for the punter. I understand the reasons for this and am an extremely guilty party myself, but a great deal of publicity seems to be aimed solely at people who are already converted to the medium.

This isn't helped by the unsynchronised nature of the industry. The publicity has to precede a show by several months since venues need to be booked well in advance of the performance date. Most shows are mere concepts in a creative imagination when the publicity is written. This means that even though there may be a major theme and a title, nothing specific can be written about the substance of the show because as yet it doesn't exist. The publicity photograph must be as abstract as possible, using a favourite object that may or may not appear in the fir-' performance.

Hype, or the 'bums on the seats at all costs' form of promotion, can be an enemy to sincere art. I don't think it is fair, either, to use forms of publicity for live art that depend on a fixed product, as with a rock group or a play. This may sell both audiences and artists short.
Roland Miller

I realise that this is all tied up with how these performances are made but it can be very infuriating for a promoter. Trying to sell an unknown show by a barely known company to a hostile public is bad enough, but trying to explain to a local paper for preview coverage is almost impossible.

Identify the event

One way to turn this into an advantage is to market the 'new', identifying the medium as live art so that the prospective punter will at least know that something challenging will be presented regardless of its form or content. Another is to promote a large event rather than one performance (as with the showcases).

While the Quarter Club was promoting at the Green Room we were also accepting commissions and designing shows as a performance group. Over these few years we have performed at several festivals throughout the country none of which have been live art events. Each show has been constructed so it can be performed in public spaces rather than theatres or galleries.

They have all been humorous, ironic pieces and would probably be described as street theatre but they have very little to do with juggling or fire eating. For an audience they are relatively easy to understand and as long as the spectators laugh they have at least made some meaning of the piece and it has been successful.

Using other events

Coming into live art from a theatre background colours your definition of what is a successful performance. The more people who see the performance the more the performance is likely to communicate. If a performance has amusing elements to it these will allow a spectator an opening and enable them to get closer to the aspects that are more serious. I think live art should jolt people from their everyday lives and bring to them a new awareness of their common surroundings. The Quarter Club has found that the most accessible way of doing this is by performing at populist carnivals and festivals.

Since these events are promoted as entertaining and fun they provide large unsuspecting audiences who may never see live art in galleries or theatres. Put in a context with market stalls, fun fairs and jugglers, our outdoor performances have reached more people than any of our showcases or individual promotions at the Green Room. This mix of live art in popular events gives the work an instant accessibility that hiding it away in established theatres and galleries doesn't achieve. This means you don't have to chase an audience and you can make use of the general publicity for the event.

On the other hand just putting live art in public spaces doesn't make it accessible. You open yourself up to some unpredictable

We made a tactical decision early on not to mention the term performance art – no one knows what it is and the funding budgets for it are minute.

Adrian Sinclair, Heads Together, Physical Theatre

situations, some of which illustrate how upset people can get when they feel threatened by something they can't make any sense of. Telling them it is live art will increase their hostility and handing them a leaflet with 50 words of absurd smug copy on it will definitely lead to violence.

Promoting is part of the event

The Quarter Club's next venture was to promote its own large scale event – a weekend festival of experimentation at the Green Room using the theatre, the foyer and the road running alongside the building. I foolishly underestimated the difference between a three hour evening showcase and a two-day and night, non-stop festival using an outdoor space and up to 20 programmed events. I learnt some lessons about budgeting, organising, teamwork, fund-raising and publicity.

These are all interlinked. Promotion is not something separate. You have to include publicity costs in your budget (design, printing, distribution, etc); you can offer sponsors a profile in leaflets and posters (you can even sell advertising in leaflets and programmes); you need to know who your audience is; you have to be able to describe the event in different ways for different people; you have to be able to co-ordinate all this. As far as possible prepare a detailed plan of how everything will run during the event, including how and where the audience fits in.

Never presume that because you understand and are attracted to the publicity everybody else will be. If you are promoting an event you think will be interesting to other people let them know about it directly, don't give them a puzzle to solve. Consider your audience.

Our most successful attempt to encourage interest in the work was a small tour of further and higher education colleges, with a short talk and slide presentation explaining as many of the diverse aspects of live art as possible. The response was very positive but 90% of the students had had no exposure to the medium at all before then.

I do enjoy live art in all its forms. It excites me intellectually and emotionally but I realise that, because of the nature of it, it will never be easily consumed. And it is a bugger to promote.

Roll up, roll up

by David Butler

A bugger though it may be, there are some simple guidelines common to all publicity.

> **I have found it very hard to get publicity and have suffered many broken promises particularly from radio and TV. The only way seems to meet the relevant person and prepare a press release in advance and send it everywhere; and then rely on luck.**
>
> Brian Morgan

One is the AIDA rule – publicity should *attract* (so it will get noticed); it should *inform* (so the audience will know who, what, where and when); it should create *desire* (ie be persuasive); and it should induce *action* (it should let the audience know what you want it to do, eg attend the show, and tell them how to do it, eg where to get tickets).

Publicity needn't cost a lot of money. The press is always free (unless you are buying advertising but for most live art events that would be a waste of time in a newspaper). If there is a free listings magazine use it. If you are sending a press release to a newspaper write it exactly as you want it to appear, enclose photographs, give a telephone number where they can contact you, address it to the right person on the newspaper (ring up and ask who that is), and then follow it up with a phone call.

Design leaflets so they can double as posters. Think about who your audience is and where to find them and then get leaflets there, either by hand or by post. Footing it round town putting up posters is usually little more than good exercise.

Use the venue's or the promoter's publicity. They will have their own leaflets, mailing lists, etc. But don't rely on it. Check what they are doing properly represents the event and do your own publicity as well if you need to. Use the venue to find out about local newspapers, radio stations, listings magazines, etc – get contact names and copy deadlines. Provide the venue with your publicity for overprinting or for a tour do a leaflet with all the tour dates on it. Include the cost of this in your fee.

> **We always find it better to be invoved in publicity – venues can write highly inappropriate things.**
>
> Anna Hayes & Glenn Davidson

And if you are performing outdoors don't forget barking. Beating a drum, singing a song, doing one piece of performance to attract a crowd to watch another, worked well for showmen and it can work for you. But remember to ask yourself what you are doing publicity for. Is it just to get a big audience or a particular audience? Your publicity represents you and your performance. It is the first introduction many people will have to your work. So don't let it misrepresent your work.

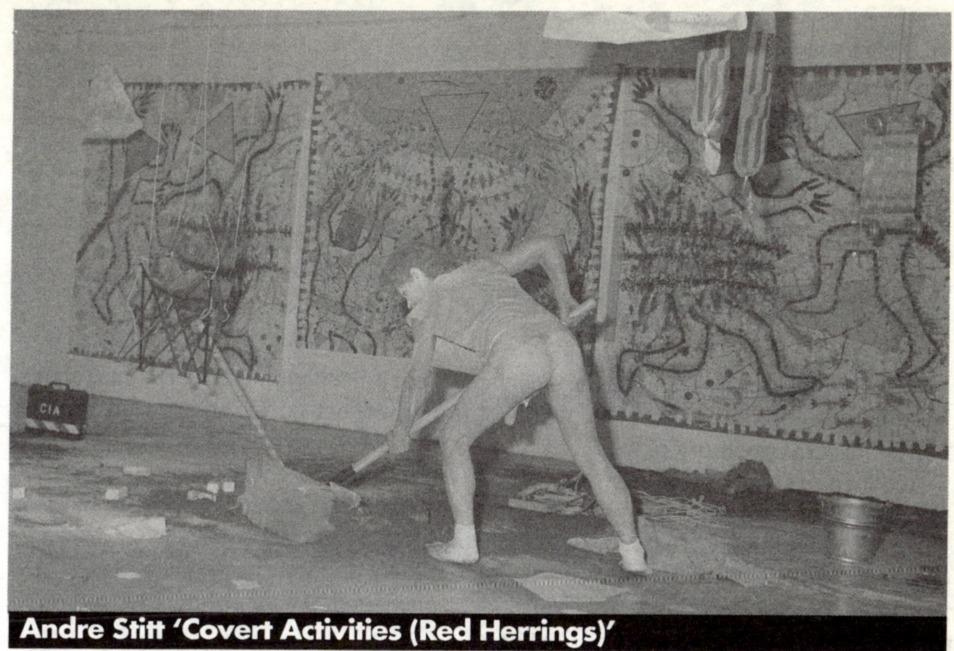

Andre Stitt 'Covert Activities (Red Herrings)'

One of the main themes in my work is that of the 'trickster', a figure one can find in many cultures. From the idea of trickster I have run a whole gamut of characters I have recognised in myself. Performances have aspects of stereotypical situations – I have become the 'Geek', the 'Hebrephenic' and the 'Akshun Man' – all elements of my own personal trickster cycle of performances or 'akshuns'. Often my work with these types and the performance structure is of a confrontational nature, both with myself and the audience.

On many occasions I have had to hire spaces and produce work and pay for all expenses and publicity. I seem to be out on a limb in this country. There has always been a safe option for promoters so, in the main, I would prefer to have full control over what I wish to do. I have organised two full coast-to-coast tours of the USA, the last in 1989, where I secured shows from Texas across the States to California for myself, Tara Babel and Shaun Caton. I have applied nine times to the British Council and have received nothing. Each time I have travelled abroad I have paid for the travel and events myself although I have been officially invited to 'name' galleries and festivals. There have been exceptions when I did not apply to the British Council – on these occasions the host venue has paid full travel, board, expenses and fee. In the States local radio programmes and interviews, cable and access TV proved very valuable in promoting events and making an otherwise ill-informed public aware of work.

Photo: Beth Ridgell. 'Covert Activities' was performed in September 1988 at the International Sculpture Conference in Dublin.

13 • Documentation

by Simon Herbert

The collective memory of my audiences serves as the best documentation for all my performances in the past. Often I encounter people who saw performances of mine done ten, twenty or even thirty years ago, who remember (sometimes better than I do) relevant aspects of my past performances. That, for me, is the true *raison d'etre* of all live art.
David Medalla

The role that documentation plays in offering an illumination into various modes of live art cannot be underestimated, yet the desire to record and re-interpret live work is often carried out at the expense of the actual event. Live art, by definition, is the 'real thing', which is experienced only by the artist and the audience: documentation of live art is merely a secondary and intermediary element, a fact often easy to ignore or misinterpret – not least by artists themselves.

An examination of documentation falls into two specific categories: how to approach capturing an event by photographic or video media; and more importantly, the potential range of meanings that can be ascribed to documentation.

Recording a live event

Basically, documenting a live event is merely a matter of common sense and sensibility, depending on both the needs of the artist and the organisation which presents the work. The list of dos and don'ts can never be completely comprehensive, as live work can take place in such a wide variety of contexts and locations: an intervention work presented by the artist alone, work made purely as a private performance, work made in conjunction with other artists and/or venues, etc. However, there are a series of considerations that can act as a general rule-of-thumb.

Most obviously the first choice facing an artist is what media to document the work in – the two primary ones are photographic and video.

Photographic documentation is certainly the cheaper of the two methods and the artist has to decide whether to use black and white negative film, or colour slides. The former is especially useful for prints for magazines, etc. The latter is better suited for talks and lectures. Another possibility is to record on colour slide and produce single black and white images from this for review purposes.

Video documentation varies greatly in expense, depending on the format used. This can range from a hand-held VHS camera, through to a fully-equipped, three-camera mixing desk and crew (in almost all cases prohibitively expensive). A factor to bear in mind is the light available during the performance; different types of camera vary enormously in their capability to adapt to low light conditions, which is usually the norm for live art. The now rather primitive three-tube cameras which have been in use for many years compare unfavourably with the more recent chip cameras which will not suffer a 'burnt' tube if pointed for any length of time at a single intense light source.

These chip cameras are specified as working at various levels of 'low-lux' lighting, the lower the lux the more sensitive the camera. Also the more recent cameras have become far more portable, useful if the performance is mobile and involves the audience changing positions.

The expense of documenting work on video does not necessarily end with the actual shoot. Post-production and editing costs can also be very expensive if the artist wants to produce a shorter version for teaching or promotional purposes. Costs vary not only between the U-matic, VHS and more recent BETA formats, but also whether the footage is of broadcast quality or not.

I find video documentation that is purely a record of a performance actually quite boring, it's often a very poor substitute for the event. So, maybe it's better to use the video record creatively, so that it becomes a piece of art in its own right.
Richard Layzell

Further expense will be incurred if documentation of British standard (PAL) needs to be transferred to foreign standards: NTSC for most of the rest of the world (particularly America and Canada) and SECAM for France.

The costing for video documentation will be carried out on an individual basis and it is up to the artist to balance quality against expense. Whatever the artist's decision, it is vital not to play the master tape too often, particularly with low grade video such as VHS, as the material degenerates substantially after only a few plays. A worthwhile precaution would be to only play the master for editing purposes or for duplicating copies that can be played more regularly.

Once a preferred medium has been identified the artist must then work out if the documentation process can actually go ahead.

Presuming most live works are presented by an artist with the support of an arts organisation, the most crucial first point to recognise is that the organisation is collaborating with the artist on the event only; it is up to the artist to decide what role, if any, documentation is to play. Consequently, areas of discussion between artist and organiser should initially establish whether documentation of the event is required by either or both parties.

Decide who will pay for the film or video stock and photographer, camera operator and sound recordist. Any initial agreement should clarify which party is responsible for the costs incurred. An artist may wish to suggest their work be documented by the organiser, but such an arrangement will probably be separate from the actual event expenditure. An organiser does not have an automatic right to document the event without the explicit permission of the artist.

Dependent on who pays for the documentation, the most crucial point to establish is who ultimately retains control of this material, and how the other party can benefit from it. This can be loosely summed up:

- If the promoter does not want to contribute to documentation costs, the artist is at liberty to separately employ someone at their own expense to record the work. Although the promoter has not contributed to the costs, it is up to the artist to consider whether copies may be made available to the promoter as a courtesy, with the rider that the promoter will cover all necessary costs (stock/ personnel) in obtaining this material.
- In the event that the promoter wishes to cover the documentation costs, chances are they want to use the resultant documentation in the future, either for archival purposes, post-publicity (reviews) or as supporting material for future funding applications.

It is up to you and the promoter to reach an agreement on the terms of this usage: basically, how you will benefit from having your work documented at no personal cost, and how the promoter will benefit from having paid for the costs.

There are no hard and fast rules for the final decision both parties will make, but whatever the outcome it should be formally acknowledged in a letter of agreement, either separate from, or as an addition to, the overall performance contract. This agreement will presumably be mutually satisfactory to both parties; once you have signed an agreement it will be legally binding.

If the promoter is paying for the cost of documentation then the contract may well also give them ownership of the material. Some questions to clarify will be:

see 17 • Copyright

- Who owns copyright. This is a separate issue to ownership of documentation and can be vital to controlling the use of documentation. There may be more than one copyright involved.
- What control can the artist expect to retain on the usage of this material? Is the promoter willing to define a set of agreed purposes of usage, beyond which written permission will be needed from the artist (eg ensuring the artist will not see solarized scratch-footage of their work on a late night arts programme, or in other situations which the artist may feel cheapens or misrepresents their original live work)? For instance, documentation may be used for archival, educational and promotional purposes only.
- If the promoter employs a free-lance company or individual to record the event, what is the agreement between them?
- What access will the artist have to this material?
- What costs will the artist be expected to incur in obtaining copies of this material, as black-and-white prints, duplications of colour slides, video formats that either correspond to, or are transferred from, the original format?
- How will the artist acknowledge this material in the event of publication or transmission and/or vice versa?

This list is by no means exhaustive. For instance, it does not take into account whether the artist wishes to ask the promoter to enforce a policy of no cameras being brought into the space by members of the audience. Neither can it possibly clarify what is a reasonable waiting time for the artist to expect to receive copies of documentation: you may very well be desperate for the promoter to send you six colour dupes and two hours of raw VHS footage as supporting material for an urgent pending application, but imagine if you were the next artist making a live work in the same festival. Would you want to be told that the promoter couldn't find the time to get your slide projector because he/she had to rush off to a processing laboratory?

In my own experience as both artist and promoter, the stringency of any final terms of agreement on documentation depends on how comfortable both the artist and promoter are in working together on that far more important element: the live work itself. If the promoter you are dealing with has no prior experience of organising live events, chances are that documentation is the last thing considered to be a priority (and rightly so); if the promoter has an ongoing history of presenting live work, chances are they will have a relative sensitivity to your needs. It is up to you to use your judgement as to how specific or not you are on this matter.

Supposing you have both managed to reach an agreement, a great deal of sensitivity is needed by both parties as to what demands the process of documentation places on the actual live work. Bluntly put, there is nothing more efficiently designed to disrupt a live event, and distract both artist and audience, than a shutter-happy photographer clicking away during the silent sections; or using a flash gun like a stroboscope light instead of using a fast film that retains the dignity of the live work (flash is definitely out for all kinds of work, unless by prior consent for informal large-scale outdoor events); or sliding out of their chair and invading the designated performance space in order to get the dramatic close-up; or a two person video/audio crew stumbling through the audience like a techno-symbiotic Siamese twin.

The list goes on. The final decision for both artist and promoter should be based on the recognition that you are dealing with live work; that work may be designed to abuse, confront, pacify or instill a sense of wonder into the viewer, but what the work should not be is a function of the documentation process.

Live art documentation

What purposes can documentation of live work serve, and do we really need it?

The desire to document something essentially intangible may at first seem perverse. After all, if an artist is attracted to a medium which both implicitly and explicitly embraces visceral live experience, and in many cases consciously rejects the art-politic of object-making, it would seem that this process should be logically followed through to a point in which the only record of the work is that of memory.

One can never regain the true feel or atmosphere of a work and perhaps this is the real value of performance work in that it exists in the time produced only, all else is residue.
Andre Stitt

A survey of live art over the last three decades would not bear this out; art journals, magazines, newspapers, funding applications, television screens, video works are peppered with recorded secondary images of the unique moment. The reasons for not bending to a purist argument are understandable. Performance art, never mind live art, has only been officially named since 1969 and according to your personal perception of the medium it either started exactly then, or extended no further back than the actions of Hugo Ball and other Dadaists at Cabaret Voltaire in Zurich 1916. It is a young medium next to the precedents of painting and sculpture, and one that needs to assert its own short history. And one cannot argue against the practical needs of artists to retrospectively judge their work (they are the only ones who never see it from 'the outside') and support future proposals and applications with examples.

A true reading of any performance documentation though can only be gained with the perspective that the image, whether static or animated, is not the same thing as the performance.

An obvious and elementary point, one might think, yet one which is frequently fudged, often because of the way we consume the density of images in our mega-visual society. Mass communication and the frozen black-and-white imagery of war journalists have conditioned us to imagine that suffering can be transmitted and vicariously 'felt' via secondary material.

Documentation of that unique moment when an artist undergoes a series of physical, spatial and often cathartic emotional transformations suffers, both in comparison with a conditioned and simulated reading of mass media iconography, and in comparison with the original art event.

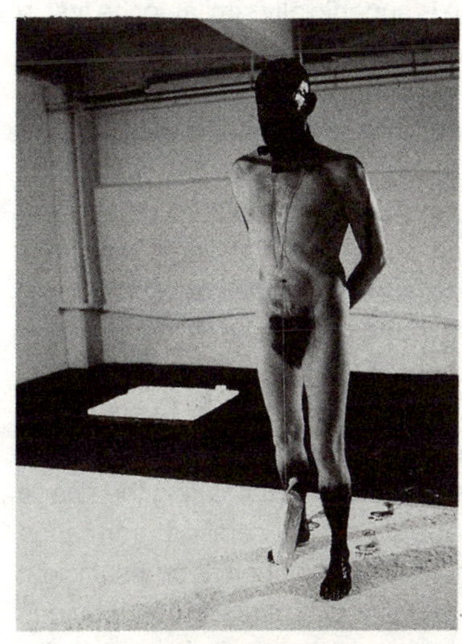

Twenty Four Hours, Alistair Maclennan, **The Basement, Newcastle, 1981.** ***Photo:*** *John Kippen*

There are both weaknesses and strengths in its function. Poor live work can be re-constituted and salvaged via good documentation, and exemplary live work can be similarly reduced. And there is nothing as boring as watching confrontational or meditative performance actions via the impartial transmitter of the video monitor.

Divorced from both fiction and reality, documentation can only be ultimately read in conceptual terms. As way of illustration, re-printed here are two photos of live actions by the artist Alastair Maclennan.

The first is a work titled 'Twenty Four Hours', presented on the 16 April 1981 at The Basement in Newcastle-upon-Tyne. From midnight to midnight, Maclennan walked in a circle between two adjacent squares of black and white flour. During this period, his action mixed and muddied the two pristine surfaces. One does not need to have been there to realise the overall implication of the work, and the metaphor that the artist was using.

The image transmits this concept for us: the action has just started, and we can see the emerging trail of his black footprints on the white flour. However, how are we to know that the action did not end at this point, with the artist standing still for the next 23 hours? The answer is that we prefer to read this as both beginning and summation; the image is the performance *in stasis*.

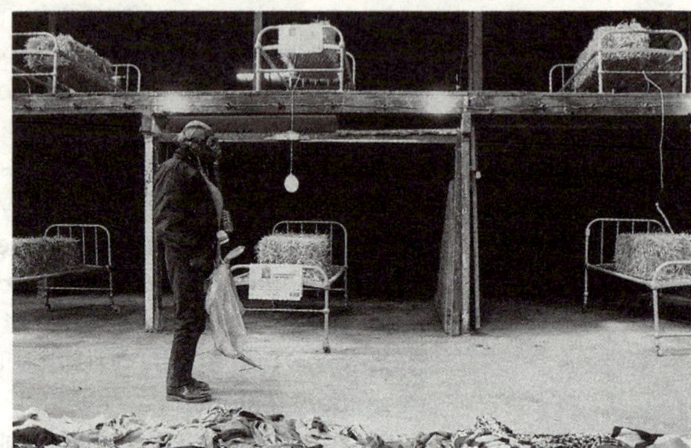

Lie to Lay, Alistair Maclennan, **New Work, Newcastle '86 festival.** ***Photo:*** *Steve Collins*

The second image is of a work titled 'Lie to Lay', presented continuously between 2-7 March 1986, at a disused warehouse, again in Newcastle-upon-Tyne. This image is superficially similar to the first; a solo figure of the artist, in situ in an environment of his own making. However, 'Lie to Lay' was not a performance that could be basically summed up by a single image. It did not consist of a singular action. Over the 120 continuous hours that Maclennan made the work, his actions included the juxtaposition of a variety of disparate objects: such as 40 bales of straw with an identical number of hospital beds, which he sporadically re-arranged; the mapping out of mutating configurations of jumble; the recording of children's hands and shoes as charcoal drawings on the walls.

Documentation is a different reality. The danger is that a viewer of documentation may believe that they have witnessed the piece itself. The essence of live work is that it is immediate and each time is unique, even if a piece is re-performed.
a. x. fraser

The lack of having experienced 'Twenty Four Hours' first-hand becomes exacerbated and magnified in acknowledging the process of assimilating the image of 'Lie to Lay'. The image still acts as codified information of the event, yet can increasingly be seen as an insufficient signifier of the event's totality. On an even more obvious level, it cannot possibly transmit the smell of the straw, the mournful audio element of a tape-loop of sheep bleating (mixed over a slowed-down version of 'Land of Hope and Glory'), the scale of all the disparate physical elements and mezzanine levels, and most importantly, the artist's attempt to supplement the conceptual side of the work with a requisite emotional response by being there as viewer or participant.

Conversely, the image of American artist Eric Bogosian performing during a series of rapidly-delivered monologues, presented at Balmbra's Music Hall in Newcastle-upon-Tyne, transmits information of a radically different kind. Other than a more visceral feel of activity and emotional charge, we are offered absolutely no clues as to the content of his work.

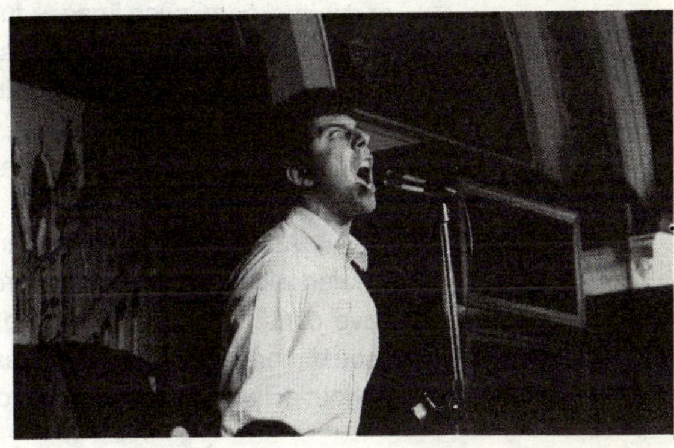

Voices of America,
Eric Bogosian, **Balmbra's Music Hall, Newcastle, 1983.**
Photo: *Steve Collins*

If we acknowledge that documentation cannot give us a complete view of live work, we can begin to acknowledge the ways in which we can extract a useful critical language and awareness of developments in live art.

Although live art has only been around for a relatively short period of time as a cultural barometer of the art world and wider world, it has bred, mutated and sub-divided into a multitude of different practices. Many artists, organisers and critics ally themselves with one area of these practices, to the conscious political rejection or exclusion of other areas. Documentation plays its part in providing critical ammunition for the worthiness of one live practice over another.

Regardless of one's personal preferences, perhaps the final point in acknowledging the mediative role of performance documentation is that live works from one decade can transmit information more effectively than that of live work from another decade. For instance, the body art prevalent in the sixties and seventies can still be read as vital and provocative in its own (photographic) right; these overtly conceptual works are compatible with the conceptual coding of the frozen image. In this respect, we can conjure up images of equal intensity to the mass-media images of the time: for the photograph of the little Vietnamese girl covered in napalm running down a highway, substitute Chris Burden, crucified on the canopy of a revving Volkswagen. For the image of a blooded and beaten Henry Cooper falling to the canvas from a punch by Cassius Clay, substitute Joseph Beuys wrapped in felt, holding out a walking stick to an inquisitive coyote.

In comparison, documentation of live work of the late seventies and eighties, which corresponds more to an abandonment of process work and an increased focus on the notion of theatrical pleasure and stimulation, does not appear as significant. Separated from a conceptual or minimal core, such images function more as promotional stills.

However far artists may shift the cultural goal-posts in the future, as particular strands and sensibilities of one type of live art practice become dominant over another, the important point to recognise is that the process of recording these actions has been, and always will be, a secondary one.

Apart from those instances in which artists have explicitly created a live work for the camera, the frozen residual 'ghosts' of live art have constantly proven elusive as a concrete interpretative aid. We should therefore not honour these ghosts, or invest meaning in them, without acknowledging this factor.

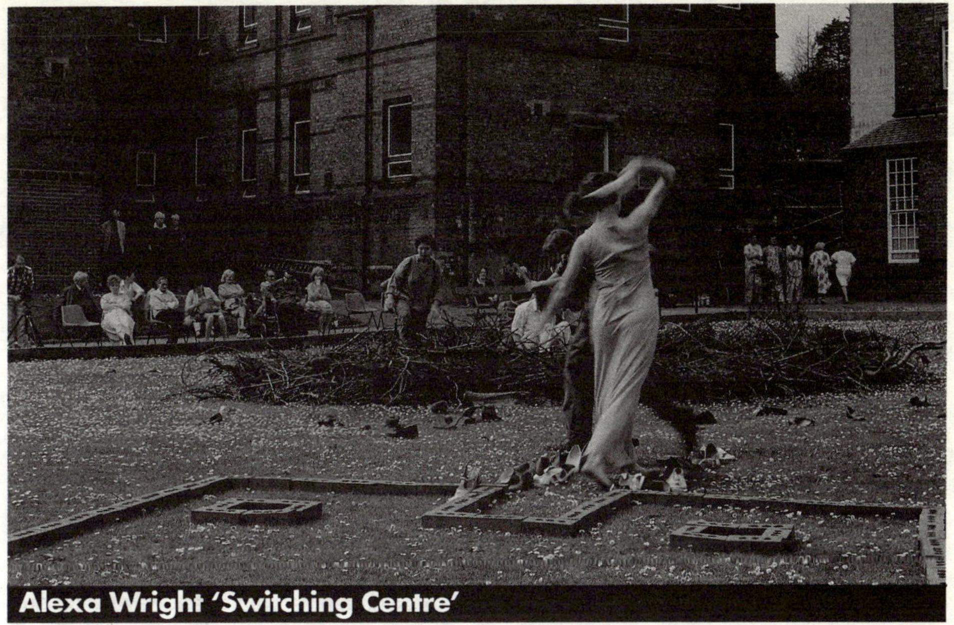

Alexa Wright 'Switching Centre'

A lot of the performances I have done have been with specific groups of people – this is a kind of research – a sharing of my ideas and practical working-out of these ideas with both artists and non-artists. I find this type of performance project very stimulating in terms of ideas for other work. There is always too little time to 'finish' a project: but I don't think this is the point. Process – the process of working with people is very important. I think a lot about audience – it is important that my work is accessible without compromising too much, a way of achieving this seems to be to involve non-artists, or young people, in its formation so that they can relate to/understand the work thoroughly. This seems, so far, to have worked quite well, although there is always an element of compromise.

I am pleased when an audience is largely non-gallery going – which they often are to these performances. In 'A foot on the Ground' made for the Ikon Gallery, Birmingham (the first I have made for a gallery situation), I filled the floor of the gallery with gravel and did not put any chairs into the gallery so that the audience had to walk in to something which started as an installation, and walk around (themselves becoming a piece of the work because of the noise their feet made on the gravel) before the action began. This worked very well. I have previously attempted a similar thing in the piece 'Fitting Images' made for the Royal Station Hotel, Newcastle. This took place in a function room and I wanted the audience to perform as though they were at a function, but whilst I was preparing the performers someone went and got chairs and by the time we began the audience was seated. Failure!

Photo: 'Switching Centre', performed with Louise Wilson, Delapole Psychiatric Hospital, Hull

14 • Funding

by Jeni Walwin

It is now only in exceptional circumstances that artists can apply to a single organisation or funding body for financial support and expect to cover all the costs of making a new work from that one application. More often than not artists will be expected to show they have, or intend to get, support from a range of sources both within the public and private sectors. It is also becoming less common for artists to receive direct financial support as individuals working on their own. The fund-raising programme itself often presents problems administratively which are difficult to manage for solo artists. In recent years artists working in all media have found it necessary to collaborate either with a 'promoter' or an 'agent' before making any requests for funding.

see 11 • Live art promoters

This is not to say that the initiative for artists' projects is no longer artist led. On the contrary, many of the most innovative projects result from artists drawing on wider support which contains administrative skills relevant to the proposed project. These collaborations may take several different forms determined by the nature of each individual project. For artists making temporary works appropriate promoters could include festivals, galleries, art centres or non venue-based promoting organisations such as Projects UK or the Film and Video Umbrella. There may also be a relationship with an agent who might either be an independent arts administrator, producer or an agency acting for artists much in the way that theatrical and literary agents have looked after the interests of practitioners. There are unfortunately few examples of commercial dealers or private sector galleries acting for artists who make live or temporary work. Indeed when these partnerships have occurred the dealers have been mostly interested in the objects which exist outside an artist's performance and around which a price tag can be more readily tied.

In this chapter I have found it useful to distinguish between the public and private sectors. It has traditionally been considered that time-based work is most likely to find financial support within the public realm.

Live and temporary work has rarely produced objects as purchasable items – much early work in this field deliberately avoided object-making, and so made itself less attractive to the commercial gallery sector which was engaged in the sale of art as permanent and fixed commodity.

In spite of the private sector's traditional hesitancy in embracing live work, it is important that the artists should not focus too exclusively on public sector possibilities when considering fund-raising. Over the last decade available funds in all public agencies have shrunk in real terms. In some cases this has not necessarily resulted in less money for performance art. Each authority or funding body is constantly reviewing its criteria for support and the so-called experimental areas can sometimes be identified as a priority.

Coincidental with the decline in public funding, several new initiatives have emerged which could offer even greater financial opportunities to artists making temporary work than the funding agencies were ever able to consider. The growth in public art commissions has yet to take on board the full implications of an artist's relationship with a site and develop the potential for time-based work. One should also mention the small but continuing commitment from television to commissioning artists' work for broadcast. Both these areas are likely to expand but much still needs to be done to alert the patrons and producers to the suitability of a wide range of work in new media to both the small screen and the great outdoors.

Public sector

The organisations and authorities discussed in this section are either distributing public funds or are supported to varying degrees by the public purse.

Arts funding agencies

The British Council

The British Council supports British art and artists overseas. Live artists have received support through both the Visual Arts and Drama Departments and through the Arts Project Unit. Artists making installations have also been supported through Visual Arts which runs two schemes: the *Grants to Artists Scheme* and the *Subsidies Scheme*.

The *Grants to Artists Scheme* is intended to encourage private and independent galleries who wish to exhibit the work of British artists, and acknowledges the important and influential links which exist between the private and publicly-funded sectors. British artists who have received a firm invitation to exhibit in a private gallery abroad may apply for assistance in meeting transport or personal travel costs. The scheme is competitive in the sense that demand outstrips the funds available and is administered by a small assessing committee which meets quarterly. It covers contemporary fine art, crafts, photography, design and architecture; about 100 individual artists are supported in a year.

The *Subsidies Scheme* is intended to complement the department's own exhibition activities by providing assistance to public museums or galleries abroad for exhibitions of British art, organised without the department's direct administrative involvement. Subsidies are generally given as a contribution towards international transport costs or the publication of a catalogue and are sometimes supplemented by the Council's overseas offices.

Both schemes operate primarily in countries where galleries and museums have the expertise and organisational capacity to work directly with artists and institutions in the UK.

The Arts Council

The Arts Council supports live art through both its drama and visual art allocations. Film and video work (including video installations) are supported through the Film, Video and Broadcast Department. A range of temporary work which has its roots in fine art thinking is supported through the Visual Arts Department.

The Visual Arts Department administers the *Live Art Commissions Scheme* which offers support to organisations wishing to commission new work in performance. Applications are considered annually and in 1990/91 approximately £30,000 was divided between five organisations which included Contemporary Archives Festival, Nottingham and the Rochdale Art Gallery.

The Art Projects Scheme embraces a wide range of support to contemporary art in all media and offers funds to organisations wishing to distribute work inter-regionally, either by exhibition, publication, conference or other special event.

In tandem with the education and training units, the department also offers support to artists taking temporary work in a number of specific ways. In 1989 and 1990 there were live art placements in art schools, traineeships for promoters and curators of live art, research projects on live art and cultural diversity. These schemes reflect the development of an overall strategy for support to contemporary art and, in response to changing need, will be reviewed each year.

We never received a grant from the Arts Council, GLAA or any artistic body.... In the end, we found it absolutely useless to fill in the millions of pages of Arts Council forms for no reward. We worked out that if we had put all the time we took filling out forms, into working at McDonalds we could have some cash instead of wasting our time.

Michael Petry: Media Arts Group

The department continues to offer revenue support to a number of galleries who in turn commission or present temporary works as part of their ongoing programme, eg Arnolfini, Bristol.

The Drama Department administers the *Drama Projects Scheme* which offers support to groups, companies, or individual theatre practitioners for the creation of new work. Artists making live work which can be seen in theatre spaces or be accommodated in a wider programme of theatre work have received support. In recent years Rose English, Gary Stevens and the Bow Gamelan Ensemble have all been successful applicants.

International Initiative Fund has supported projects like the Edge Biennale which in turn offers significant opportunities for artists from both the UK and abroad to present temporary installations and performances in a variety of venues in Britain and Europe.

The New Collaborations Fund 1991/92 is available to artists, companies, galleries, producers, publishers and promoters to encourage new forms of collaboration between artists working in different art forms in equal partnerships, and to support the development of inter-disciplinary work. It assists the inter-disciplinary work of culturally diverse artists and organisations and emerging new multi-disciplinary art forms. The fund offers £200,000 in 1991/92 and is be available for one-off projects. Grants are offered in the forms of:

- Research and development grants
- Project production grants

The Scottish Arts Council

The Council offers direct support to artists in all media through:

- *Project Assistance Grants* (maximum £3,000)
- *Bursaries* (maximum £5,000)
- *Major Bursaries* (maximum £10,000)
- *Small Assistance Grants* (maximum £500).

It also offers direct and indirect support through a variety of schemes operated by the Awards and Exhibitions Panels: exhibitions, traineeships, artist's placements, commissions, purchases for the SAC collection, etc. Emphasis is given within some of these to 'New Projects' especially conceived to support the presentation of work outside the gallery. In 1990 such support ranged from a research grant of £1,000 to Windfall '91, to £6,000 to the staging of Edge 90 in Glasgow.

The Welsh Arts Council

Although the Visual Arts Department began 1991/2 with a general 'project' fund, it was spent by the end of May. (Two performance groups received just under 10% of the £13,500 total available). Grants to artists apply to all disciplines and include travel and masterclass awards from a fund of £24,000. Interest free loans of up to £1,000 are also available. Artists whose work is relevant to specific galleries' programmes should contact them direct. Welsh regional arts associations also advertise residencies which could include live art.

Regional arts boards

As from October 1991 the regional arts associations are known as regional arts boards and will be reduced from twelve to ten. In the main RAB's support work made or presented in their region. The following information was gathered in conversations with each RAB during the summer of 1991. It should be remembered that, like all arts funding agencies the RAB's will be constantly reviewing policies and establishing new priorities for grant aid. This information below was obtained in response to two general questions and a request for examples of each: what financial support (either direct or indirect) do you offer to artists making live or temporary works of art; what systems exist for dealing with work which cuts across artistic disciplines?

The schemes offered by the regional arts boards are liable to change, particularly at the time of this book going to press because of the structural changes taking place. The information contained here cannot represent more than an indication of the types of schemes and level of funding which has been available in the past. For up-to-date information and advice contact your local RAB directly.

see 20 • Contacts

Eastern Arts Board

The Film and Photography Department offers three sources of direct support:

- *Film and Video Exhibitions and Events Fund*
- *Film and Video Production Fund*
- *Photography Bursaries*

In the Visual Arts Department the support is offered indirectly through three channels:

- *Signposts Scheme:* eg Rhona Lee in residence at the Junction, Cambridge – a new venue for live music and performance

Due to my work being puppet figure based the live art structure, particularly with funding, has rejected my proposals. The grounds for refusal have been 'she uses puppets therefore she's 'drama'. Such attitudes are a great restriction on producing work which does not fit neatly into prescribed definitions.
Nenagh Watson

- *Art in Public Places Scheme:* eg Sculpture in the Park, Eastern Arts Association/Cambridge Festival, exhibitions and events
- *Revenue Clients:* eg Kettles Yard and Cambridge Darkroom have both included live and temporary work in their programme
- *Visual Arts Development Fund:* considers applications which develop the artform within policy priority areas.

The Performing Arts Department will also look at applications from performance artists working closer to a theatrical tradition. Eastern Arts and Anglia TV are collaborating on a programme to be broadcast in 1992 featuring the work of four live artists at an early stage of their career.

East Midlands Arts Board

The Media and Publishing Arts Department offers two forms of direct support:

- *Starter Grants Scheme:* offers upwards of £250 to artists who have been out of college for at least three years.
- *Project Grants:* for between £500 and £750 are offered to artists embarking on new work.

In 1990/91 the total allocation for these two schemes was £8,000. Indirect support is offered through programme subsidy to, for example, the Bonington Gallery at Nottingham Polytechnic and to the Northamptonshire Library Service which recently commissioned Richard Layzell. There may be new details relating to new grant aid schemes for 1992/93 onwards – contact the Visual Arts Officer

London Arts Board

London-based events were funded by Greater London Arts. This has been replaced by London Arts Board which will work within the board outlines of the GLA strategy until LAB's own policies are in place by spring 1992. In 1991/92 a high proportion of GLA awards to individuals went to visual artists working in the time-based area. A number of GLA revenue clients are funded particularly for their installation work, eg Matts and Chisenhale Galleries. Artangel has been supported on a project basis for site-specific public work in London, and is now a revenue client. Edge has received a major one-off project award to develop a London focus for their future festivals. Within the GLA region (more than elsewhere in the UK) there has been evidence of introducing time-based artists into the public arts field working through agencies such as the Public Art Development Trust.

Northern Arts Board

The visual arts department offers four forms of direct support to artists:

- *Visual Arts Awards:* total allocation in 1991/92 £14,500, maximum individual award £2,000
- *Annual Bursary for individual artist:* current award £7,000.
- *Travel and Training Scheme*
- *Interest-free loans*

Live and temporary art is supported indirectly through Northern Arts allocation to Projects UK – a key strategic organisation in the north. In 1990, with support from Northern Arts, Edge presented their opening programme in a number of sites in Newcastle.

Arts Board North West

The Visual Arts Department offers direct support to artists through two schemes:

- *Training Bursaries and Fees for Community Workshops*
- *Revenue Clients:* most notably Horse and Bamboo received £54,430 in 1990/91

Indirect support is offered through: *Project Funding*, eg showcase performances at the Green Room; and *Revenue Clients*, eg Cornerhouse who jointly commissioned a performance and installation from Silvia Ziranek in 1990/91.

Southern Arts Board

Until 1990/91 the Visual Arts Department maintained a separate budget for project support to performance art, but this is now dealt with as part of the overall Visual Arts budget. In 1990/91 direct support has been offered to an artists' group at Open Hand Studios in Reading for a series of presentations. Indirect support is offered through galleries such as Aspex in Portsmouth which has maintained an occasional commitment to live and temporary work. Of the many mixed discipline festivals several are now being encouraged to incorporate non-gallery based visual arts into their programmes. Cross departmental support to mixed discipline projects is response based, there is no strategy except where curriculum development in schools is concerned.

South East Arts Board

The Drama Department offers direct support to performance art groups, eg Theatre of Whitstable. Indirect subsidy is given through support of annual clients, eg the Zap Club in 1990/91 received £9,000 to support performance art events. The James Hockey Gallery at West Surrey College of Art and Design has received project support for installation/performance work. There have been several successful examples of joint funding with the Dance Department, eg Liz Aggis and Etheldredra, and there is potential for further cross funding with Visual Arts of installation and performance work under the general heading of *Contemporary Initiatives*.

South West Arts Board

In the Visual Arts Department direct support is offered through:

- *Annual Awards:* one fellowship and four project awards, 1990/91 allocation £7,000
- *Training and Marketing Awards:* maximum individual award £200. Indirect support is offered through
- *General Projects Budget:* eg the Magdelena Project at the Arnolfini (£1,000) and Semi Ambulant for a site-specific work in Bristol

In 1990/91 funds were also put aside for research and development in performance art. On cross art form projects the Assistant Director will nominate a lead officer and the relevant departments will liaise, eg Forkbeard Fantasy received joint funding from Theatre, Video and Visual Arts.

West Midlands Arts Board

There are no art form budget headings, all subsidies are allocated under:

- *Local Promoters:* eg Lanchester Gallery programme support and artists groups
- *Community Projects*
- *New Work and Production:* includes commissions, residencies, exhibitions, eg Marty St James and Anne Wilson 'Civic Monument' project, Birmingham. Within this section WMA sees it as a priority to encourage cross art form collaborations, eg 'Fine Rats', 'Collective Art Noise'
- *Training*
- *Marketing*

New arts strategies are being developed to be in place by early 1992.

Yorkshire and Humberside Arts Board

In the Visual Arts Department direct support is offered for 50% of total costs through

- *Individual Awards:* maximum £500, total allocation 1991/92 £10,000, including Visual Arts, Crafts and Performance Art Individual grants
- Performance Art Events: individuals or organisations touring to one venue in the region, should also demonstrate active education programme. Total allocation 1991/92 £1,500
- *Training:* marketing and contemporary issues in visual arts and crafts are particularly targeted 1991/92 £10,000

Indirect support is offered through annual clients, eg Kirklees Art Space. In exceptional cases projects can be funded from more than one department.

Local authorities

Indirect support to artists making live and temporary work is made available through three different channels of local authority activity.

Arts and entertainments departments

Some local authorities run their own arts programmes and a few consider live art to be a part of that programme, eg Nottingham City and Nottinghamshire which host an annual festival 'Contemporary Archives' devoted to performance art and Nottinghamshire which also operates a Commissions Programme called New Arts Work, and Southampton where two successful festivals of performance have occurred.

Try to avoid purely specialist arts funding and go instead for social services, town planning, education, youth funding, health, environmental sources. Get to know your location (either by living there, or through thorough research), and stick to your own ideas, instead of getting enmeshed in some arts administrator's project for career enhancement.
Roland Miller

Galleries and museums

Curators and exhibition organisers are beginning to incorporate non-object-based work into their programmes of temporary exhibitions, eg Harris Museum, Preston presented 'Acts of Remembrance' in 1989 and the Laing Art Gallery, Newcastle collaborated with Projects UK on 'New Work: Newcastle' a season of performance and installation work in 1988 and 1989.

Public art

Some local authorities have adopted a percent for art scheme on all capital developments. Birmingham and Oxfordshire are cases in point. As yet few commissions have been offered to artists making live work.

The education sector

Most support has come from the tertiary sector where artists have been involved in teaching, residencies and performance programmes. However the primary sector, with its openness to cross discipline work has begun to successfully introduce live artists to residencies and workshops, eg Richard Layzell, Handsworth Junior School, Birmingham, 1988. Support to performance from within polytechnics and colleges of art can be divided into three areas.

Because of its implicit rejection of traditional notions of form and content, its integration of theory and practice and its relationship with 'art' and 'life', live art has a valuable place in our education system.
Lois Keidan, ACGB Live Art discussion paper, 1991

Permanent & visiting staff

Employment of performance artists is rare, but Newcastle has a continuing commitment for the practice amongst its visitors and Nottingham, Wimbledon, Dartington, Wolverhampton, Brighton and Sheffield all have artists making live work on their permanent staff.

Programmes of performance work

Through its Powerhouse season Nottingham Polytechnic has presented a regular programme of performance for theatre spaces. Brighton Polytechnic has occasionally collaborated with the Zap Club and the Brighton Festival on performance seasons for its Salis Benney Theatre.

Residencies

see 3 • Personal histories

Residencies are less common in polytechnics now, but both the Film and Video and the Visual Arts Departments at the Arts Council have in the past funded placements for artists in order to encourage debate and heighten awareness of the potential for live and time-based work beyond the art school context.

Independent arts organisations

see 11 • Live art promoters

The following organisations will not give artists funds to pursue their own work in isolation but many of them will work with artists to raise funds to commission new work, to administer tours of performances, and to arrange for marketing and educational programmes appropriate to the live work.

Arts centres

These venues are traditionally more open to cross discipline work. The ICA, London and the Third Eye, Glasgow have regularly commissioned new work in performance from the UK and worldwide.

Galleries

Independent galleries such as the Ikon in Birmingham and the Museum of Modern Art in Oxford are regularly including performance and installation work in their yearly programmes.

Theatres

The Green Room in Manchester has had a regular commitment to live art and the Purcell Room on London's South Bank is beginning to develop a small element of live art within its programme and the Traverse Theatre, Edinburgh shows a continuing interest in the practice.

Festivals

From amongst the country's large mixed discipline festivals little attention has been given to live art, although Edinburgh did recently include the Wooster Group and Archaos in its international programme. Brighton has worked consistently with a number of East European performance groups and Glasgow 1990 collaborated with Edge to present a number of international performance and installation pieces.

Non-venue-based organisations

Amongst these, Projects UK in Newcastle and Hull Time Based Arts have been responsible for commissioning much of the new live art seen in the UK.

National events

Single discipline festivals and experimental events of national significance have been responsible for raising the profile of much performance, live art and installation work in recent years.

- The National Review of Live Art: now in its tenth year, platforms of new work in performance, commissioned artists, has moved from Nottingham to Glasgow.
- Edge 88 and Edge 90: commissioned new work in installation, performance and video, London, Newcastle and touring.
- TSWA3D and TSW Four Cities Project: site-specific, non-gallery installations commissioned from international artists.
- LIFT (London International Festival of Theatre): now in its tenth year, the British contribution to the programme is often made by performance and live artists.

Agencies

- The Artangel Trust is interested in working with visual artists in any discipline (sculpture, dance, music, live art, etc) in relation to particular sites, places, or public contexts.

- ArtsAdmin works with a range of performance artists and new theatre groups helping to fund-raise, administer tours and arrange publicity.
- Public Art Forum comprises a number of agencies specifically concerned with the commissioning of art for public places.

Public organisations & institutions with occasional arts programmes

Whilst not primarily concerned with promoting the arts the following organisations have introduced art into their regular programmes and will occasionally consider including work by time-based artists: health authorities, tourist boards, the prison service, organisations for people with special needs, eg Shape, and the Commission for Racial Equality.

The private sector

Commercial galleries and dealers

In the introduction to this chapter I referred to the uncomfortable relationship which has predominated between temporary works and commercial spaces but there are a small number of dealers who have in one way or another supported artists who make live art or installation pieces. The focus of attention within these galleries has usually been on the objects that relate to temporary works rather than temporary works themselves. There are exceptions. Nigel Greenwood was amongst the first to present performances by Gilbert and George in his gallery in the early seventies. Anthony D'Offay has consistently shown objects and installations by Joseph Beuys and Bruce McLean. More recently Marlene Eleini has worked with Helen Chadwick and Andrea Fisher. Anthony Reynolds has worked with Silvia Ziranek on performances and installations, and amongst the group of artists showing with Mario Flecha and Interim Art are some whose focus is on live, temporary or site-specific work. Although these examples have often resulted in some financial benefit for the artists, it has rarely involved payment for live work.

Pubs & clubs

Some kinds of work are suitable for presentation in non-art contexts and can generate income from these alternate sources. The Zap Club in Brighton is perhaps the most obvious example of a club which has successfully integrated a range of performance styles into its weekly programmes. On a smaller scale but equally successful in its time was the Pink Room in Loughborough. The Limelight Club in London's Charing Cross Road has also played occasional host to performance artists.

Sponsors

The most common form of sponsorship offered to performance artists has been in kind, where equipment or materials have been loaned or given for use in a specific event. Very few of the regular art sponsors have been interested in the association with experimental or innovative work which the sponsorship of live art would imply. However, there are exceptions. Thames TV funded an entire season of new performance at the ICA entitled the 'Ripple Effect', Becks Bier have sponsored several installations and performance events and Barclays New Stages programme is specifically designed to support new work in theatre. For a detailed analysis of arts funding from industry, please refer to Chapter 14 of 'The Arts Funding Guide' by Anne-Marie Doulton, published by the Directory of Social Change, 1989.

see 21 • Further reading

Trusts & foundations

Amongst grant-making trusts which offer support to the arts The Calouste Gulbenkian Foundation has been the most notable source of support. Its current priorities include regeneration and development, cultural equity and arts in rural areas. For a more detailed analysis of grant-making trusts see Chapter 13 of 'The Arts Funding Guide', as above.

Broadcast

Within the last two years artists making performances have contributed to 'Club X' (Channel 4), 'The Late Show' (BBC 2) and the 'Bette Midler Show' (BBC 1). Videos have been commissioned from a range of artists (many of whom make performance work) for '19:4:90 – Television Interventions' (Channel 4) and, in a joint initiative from the 'Late Show' and the Arts Council, artists have been commissioned to make innovative short works for 'Artists One-Minute Television'.

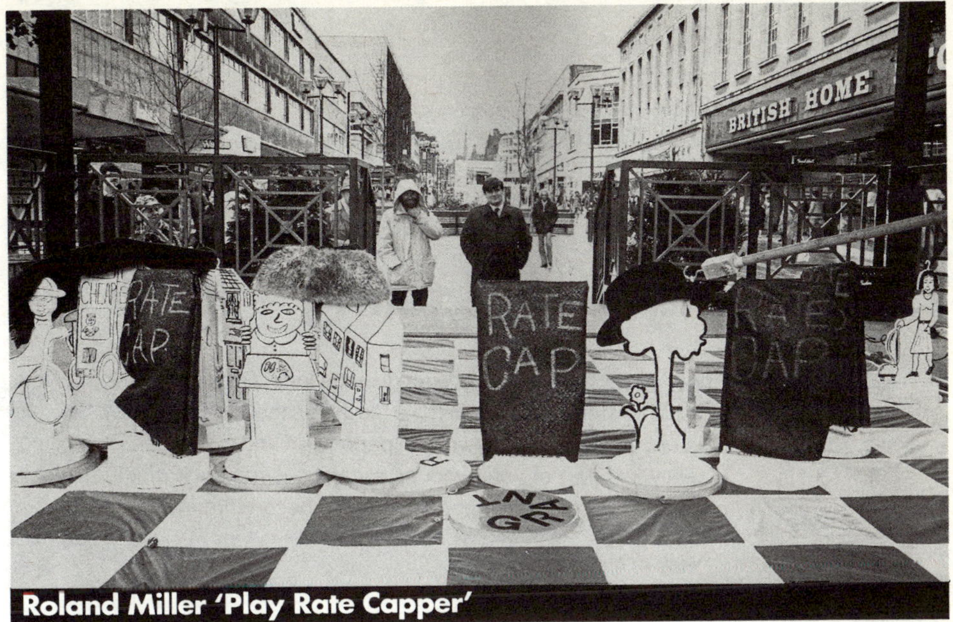

Roland Miller 'Play Rate Capper'

'Play Rate Capper' was commissioned by Sheffield City Council Education Department to support the campaign against the government's rate capping legislation. This commission would now be illegal.

I don't find it difficult to arrange work outside recognised venues. My current work in Glasgow, and previous work there, fits in with perceptions of art as a part of social service. The problems come with the specialist arts funding bodies and individuals. I would rather work with non-arts structures because, as a friend who organises public art projects in France puts it: *'better to work with planning authorities, instead of arts authorities, because the planning authorities think of social, environmental factors, whilst the arts people only apply artistic values'.* Basically, arts administrators believe they are the only people empowered to place work, and they are hostile to an artist who takes it into his/her own hands. This is one of my objections to the recent trends in live art funding. I also object to the kudos given to institutional promotions over and above anything done by an individual artist.

Starting at the Devon County Show in 1972, and over the subsequent seven years Shirley Cameron and I visited shows all over England and Scotland. We made all the arrangements ourselves, involving the RAAs only for money and some publicity. It worked very well. Spectators could be counted in the hundred's of thousands and the siting of our tent, next to beasts, machinery, seed demonstrations, etc was excellent. We found it very relaxed, and the public in a good mood to talk with us and discuss art . We only stopped doing agricultural shows because we wanted a change, and we moved to the city.
Photo: Jerry Millman

15 • Pricing & budgeting

by David Butler Prices, fees, budgets. These are like the letters from the bank that you hide behind the bread bin. But like the letters they don't go away. Sooner or later you have to sit down with paper, pen and calculator. But pricing is really just part of your work as an artist. If you think of it that way it becomes less difficult, though it may not become more enjoyable!

Budgeting

Any budget depends on being able to estimate future costs. You will break these costs down into a series of headings (budget heads), eg fees, transport and materials. This is easier for some of your budget heads than others. The difficulties lie first in being able to accurately predict how much time is needed on an event, what materials are needed, etc. In other words, estimating 'amounts'. Having done this you should then be able to put a cost on these amounts. But you then have a problem of predicting a cost that may change over time – for instance an increase in petrol prices.

Estimating the 'amounts' obviously becomes easier with time. Experience allows you to be much clearer about what will be needed for a particular event – did you get it right last time, was there something you forgot? Because the nature of live art means that for many artists each event is different, you may not be able to make a direct comparison from one to another. But you can use your experience to develop a personal 'formula'. You get to know when working on your own a minimum preparation time of three days is needed for a one-day event, and the preparation isn't any greater for a week's event. But if you are working with three other people you need to allow another two days preparation time. You know that most of your materials can be got for nothing but that it is always useful to allow £50 as a materials budget 'just in case'.

Similarly you can adopt a formula for estimating costs. If you are budgeting for an event next month then costs of materials, accommodation, etc can be predicted accurately. But if you are budgeting for a year's time you can simply add a percentage on to allow for price increases – say 10%.

The important point is to be as realistic as possible. The worst situation is to under-budget, but also avoid over-budgeting. Don't add a bit on to all your budget heads 'just in case'. Be as accurate as possible for fees, transport, materials, etc and have an extra budget head for contingency. Either allow a fixed amount for contingency or, preferably, do it as a percentage of the total cost.

It is useful to compare the actual costs of a project with the budgeted costs. After the event this allows you to see if you estimated properly so you can do it better next time. During the event it allows you to see if you are overspending and so have to economise or do more fund-raising. If it is an event with a lot of planning, keeping say a monthly record of actual spending against the budget could be vital.

Time scales

Never underestimate the potential for things to take longer than you thought. It may seem obvious when you list it on paper that your itinerary of collection points for materials can be driven round in two hours but allow yourself some contingency here as well. It might mean when you go to photocopy your leaflets only to find the photocopier not working, you still have time to make it to another copyshop. Or it may mean after you have collected all your materials and are completely exhausted you actually have time for a cup of tea!

Things always take far longer than you expect them to.... Six weeks seems a reasonable period for developing a piece with a group of people.
Alexa Wright

Time, as they say, means money. And though you may, foolishly, find yourself forced to put in more time for no money, you can't expect others to do the same. If you are hiring in some scaffolding to be erected at 9am, you have to be sure you can get access to the site at 9am – or end up with your scaffolders going away to work on another job and coming back when the people with the PA want to put it on the scaffolding.

Time-scales need to be worked out fairly precisely, it is best done before you budget as the time taken to do something influence's the cost.

Pricing your time

Some things such as materials can be priced fairly accurately. It is pricing your own time which seems most difficult and time is the basic element in pricing live art. This is another area for having a 'formula'. In 'Fact Pack see 21 • Further reading

1 Rates of Pay', from AN Publications, Susan Jones gives the following four simple pointers to working out an hourly rate:

- Add up all your overhead costs (studio rent, rates, insurances, repairs and renewals, running a vehicle, publicity, accountancy, telephone, stationery, etc). Divide this by the number of weeks you wish to work in a year (usually no more than 47) to get a weekly overheads cost.
- Work out what you need to draw from your business account to pay for mortgage/rent, food, clothing, holidays, entertainment, etc and divide this by the number of weeks too.
- Add an annual contingency sum per week to cover unexpected costs.
- Adding the three elements gives a weekly rate; divide each by the number of hours you wish to work each week to get an hourly rate.

You can use this hourly rate to cost out any event but there are two important points to remember:

- When working out the cost for a one day event you have to take into account all the time involved to put that event together. So if a one day event lasting ten hours has taken a total of fifty hours to prepare and perform, and your hourly rate is £10, the total cost for it is £500 not £100.
- You have worked out your rate on the assumption that because you work for 48 weeks in the year you can earn for 48 weeks. If you can only earn for 24 weeks, you are going to have to double your rates.

You live and work in a market economy. So you have to accept that, though you know how you need to cost your time, a promoter may not be willing to pay that. There may be a going rate that bears no relation to your costs. There may be a difference between what a well-known artist and a newly-established artist can charge. You will probably have to do some soul searching and compromising when it comes to fees. But don't allow yourself to be browbeaten into undercharging. You are a professional. Make it clear what your real costs are. Make sure, if you are accepting a lower fee, the promoter knows what you are doing and why. You will not be alone in this. Artists are some of the biggest sponsors of the arts. You can be acknowledged as a sponsor alongside other funders.

We did get sponsorship from British Airways, Continental Airlines and many more private firms.... Funding was always a problem, but all the members chipped in from their own funds, because we wanted to make performance art. We did get help from companies who gave us goods, or services.
Michael Petry: Media Arts Group

Budget heads

Your list of budget heads should be as simple and short as possible, eg:

- Fee including costs of preparation and development time, site/preliminary visit, etc
- Transport
- Accommodation
- Materials and equipment
- Labour/technical costs
- Direct site costs, eg electrical supply, running water, Portaloos
- Publicity
- Documentation
- Contingency.

The simpler it is, the easier it will be for you to draw up and the easier it will be for other people to understand. Simplicity and clarity are key factors with figures. Don't try to acquire complex accounting skills. Use common sense and the arithmetic you learnt at school.

Budgets & proposals

The way you budget for yourself is not always the way you want to present figures to someone else.

With a promoter, for instance, you may just want to quote a fee, possibly with travel and accommodation as the only other itemised costs. Otherwise you may find a promoter haggling about the cost of materials (or who the materials belong to) after the event.

With a funder you usually have to be very precise about breaking down a budget and they can often want a different set of budget heads to the ones you have used. They may even have a form to fill in with the budget heads listed on it. There is not a lot you can do about this except a bit of creative accounting – eg if there isn't a heading for contingency split it up and add it to other budget headings. But it is worth pointing out to a funder that their grant application forms bear no relation to the way an artist really sets up a project and why it doesn't.

Presenting a budget as part of a proposal to a promoter, commissioner or funder is a bit of marketing. Just as you have to think about what will capture a potential audience's imagination when promoting an event, so you have to think about what the promoter wants to see when they read your budget and proposal.

First of all interest them either in the proposed event or in yourself. Have a simply written, brief description of the event which is going to interest the reader. Do a similar description of yourself and past work, including photographs, postcards, videos and reviews. Then give an outline of the proposed event as detailed as possible – where it will be (or what space is needed for it), how long it will take including preparation time, how many people are involved, what technical help is needed, technical specifications (electricity supply, special equipment needed), etc. Then present your budget. Offer to supply further information if needed and show clearly who is to be contacted, where and how.

Fees

by Lois Keidan

The number of variables in the production and presentation of live art make it very difficult to establish consistent rates on fees and expenses and the terms and conditions of contracts – a performance may last five minutes, five hours or five days, it may require a lot of materials and equipment or it may require none, it may involve only one artist or it may be an ensemble work for 20 people.

Any guidelines must take as their starting point these variables and encourage promoters and artists to be as flexible as the work itself demands. The following fees reflect the best of current practice. For a more detailed listing showing actual examples of the range of fees currently used throughout the UK for different forms of work see AN Publications' 'Fact Pack 1: Rates of Pay'.

see 21 • Further reading

Performances of existing works

For a one-off performance of an existing work by a solo artist a minimum fee of £200 would reflect the best current practices. Repeats or runs of performances would be at this rate or at a ceiling fee mutually agreed by artist and promoter.

For an existing but one-off collaboration between two or more artists, the artists and promoter should mutually agree whether a fee per performer will apply or whether there is a ceiling fee for the collaboration.

For a one-off performance of an existing work by a live art ensemble/group a minimum fee of £500 would reflect the best current practices. Repeats of performances would be at this rate or at a ceiling fee mutually agreed by the group and promoter.

Commissioning a new work

see 'Budget heads' above

The artist(s) and promoter should mutually agree a budget for realisation and production costs.

In addition to production costs, the best current practices suggest the promoter should pay a fee for the premiere and any additional performances on the minimum rates set out above for existing works. Relevant production costs should be paid to the artist(s) in full on signature of a contract and prior to commencement of work.

Workshops

Fees for workshops should be in addition to performance and commission fees and current practice suggests the following minimum rates:

- £100 – full-day workshop
- £75 – half-day workshop or lecture involving preparation work
- £40 – talk not involving preparation.

The promoter should also meet any promotional and incidental costs of a workshop and provide and pay for any materials used by participants.

Expenses

The performance, workshop and commissioning fees referred to above do not include travel, accommodation and subsistence costs for which additional payment should be made.

The artist(s) and promoter should always confirm in writing as part of a contract the conditions applying to travel, accommodation and subsistence.

Travel

Current practice suggests in addition to fees the promoter should cover artists' travel expenses by one of the following means:

- Provide or reimburse artists for the cost of a second class rail ticket and any necessary local transport costs (taxis should only be used if essential).
- Pay mileage allowance where own transport is used at a rate of approximately 35p per mile.
- Reimburse the artist(s) for the cost of transport hire inclusive of petrol, insurance, etc (in the case of a group this is obviously much cheaper).

It is recognised that often promoters cannot additionally pay travel expenses, in which case the artist(s) and promoter should mutually agree this and negotiate an appropriate fee taking this area of cost into account.

Claims should always be supported by receipts and should be made within one month of incurring the costs.

Accommodation & subsistence

Current practice suggests in addition to fees the promoter should also cover accommodation and subsistence costs by one of the following means:

- Reimburse the actual cost of accommodation and meals with claims supported by receipts.
- Provide and pay for clean, accessible and comfortable accommodation and provide substantial refreshments for the duration of the visit (with groups, rooming requirements must always be confirmed in advance).
- Pay subsistence at the following rates:
  - more than 5 hours but less than 10 – £3.90
  - more than 10 hours – £8.60
  - 24 hours in London – £68.50
  - 24 hours outside London – £63.15.

It is recognised that promoters cannot always pay subsistence and sometimes even accommodation costs, in which case the artist(s) and promoter should mutually agree this and negotiate a fee taking these areas of cost into account.

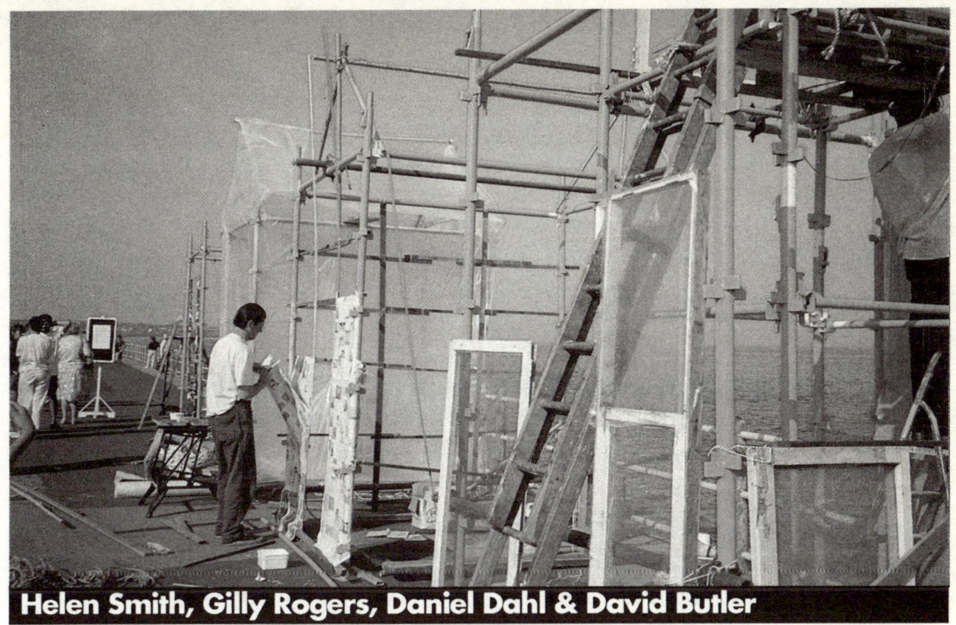

Helen Smith, Gilly Rogers, Daniel Dahl & David Butler

'Doing it ourselves' was a day-long performance/installation at the 'Waterfront Festival' in Sunderland, August 1991. Visual arts is a big part of the festival with probably forty artists taking part. The work includes participatory events, exhibiting, stalls, demonstrations, selling and performance. There is a large and varied audience, some there just for the festival, some for a day out at the seaside, so it is a good place for a live art event if you want direct interaction with your audience. 'Doing it ourselves' was a dialogue between us and passersby about houses and how we use them, about what we were doing and why.

Planning started several months in advance. We made a verbal proposal but by the time we put it on paper the festival budget was fixed. Our event had grown from three people to four. It involved hiring scaffolding. We had sold our van and had to make use of the festival van along with a lot of other artists. The festival had budgeted for a one-day event for three people with no preparation time and a fixed amount for materials. The real budget was over twice what they had allowed so we compromised to do the event. We paid for the scaffolding out of the total budget, then split the remainder into four; each of us paid for our own materials out of our 'split' and traded off with the others as necessary.

Photo: Julia Linstead

16 • Contracts

by Juliet Burgess

A contract is an agreement between two or more people which is legally binding. There are three essential ingredients:

- Agreement – one person has made a firm offer which the other has accepted.
- An intention to create a legal relationship – this is automatically presumed in a commercial agreement.
- Consideration – this is the price or something of value in the eyes of the law, such as a promise in return for a counter-promise.

Verbal agreements

A contract need not be in writing to be legally valid, apart from a few notable exceptions such as house purchase and credit agreements, provided it contains the three elements mentioned above. A verbal agreement made at a meeting or over the telephone will be legally enforceable but the advantages of committing the terms to paper are manifold. Almost all transactions in the business, theatrical and musical worlds are conducted using written contracts and there is no need for live art to be an exception. Written contracts provide:

> **We have learned through bitter experience. Always get a contract!**
> Claire Spafford: Glory what Glory

- A checklist and points of reference
- A professional framework to a business relationship
- Proof as to what was agreed should a dispute arise
- An opportunity for the parties to concentrate on the nature of the transaction and their mutual obligations.

What form should a contract take?

A written contract need not be a formal document to be valid. The contractual terms may perfectly well be contained in a letter detailing what was agreed.

During a telephone conversation take a note of the points covered and at the end read them back to the other person to ensure there is a mutual understanding of what has been agreed. Then confirm those points in a letter as soon as possible afterwards.

Use of a standard contract, (ie the same basic form each time with only details relating to venue, date, fee and so on changing) will save time re-negotiating all the basic conditions for each separate engagement. It also ensures no important point is omitted as it serves as a memorandum of terms to be covered and provides the artist with maximum protection as the terms will be largely in their favour.

The artist's position

In theory it is easy to advocate the use of the artist's own contract but in reality this may prove to be very difficult especially for the young and inexperienced. The problems are apparent, inequality of bargaining power, lack of confidence, and fear of being considered difficult to work with and not worth engaging now or in the future. You have something valuable to offer and by adopting a professional basis to working relationships in the form of a contract you are not undermining the value or quality of what you do or are trying to say. Insisting on working only with a contract is not being difficult but business-like. This is not at variance with creative integrity. Taking the initiative with a contract will in the short term provide you with more room to manoeuvre and in the long term generally improve the working conditions and expectations of the live artist.

A mutually agreed contract is a vital pre-production that establishes the aims and intentions of the commission, responsibilities entailed and the working parameters for both parties.

Lois Keidan, ACGB Live Art Strategy Discussion Paper 1991

Guidelines for working with collaborators

To impose a contract on collaborators working on a joint venture may seem inappropriate, heavy handed and destined to remove all good will. But informal agreement in advance as to how the parties will work together will help achieve a good working relationship and the right conditions to create exciting and effective art.

'A good relationship doesn't just come about by both sides being completely compatible, because that ignores the benefits of

Norman Leach, 'Contract in Writing' by Richard Pinner commissioned by the Gulbenkian Foundation, published 1984

creative conflict. What we need are some elementary rules that help make that conflict creative – a bit like marriage guidance....'

Get to know one another

Collaborators may be working together for the first time so it is valuable to set aside time to talk, share views about work, discuss experiences and interests, and establish if you can work together.

The creative process

In order to decide how the creative process will work, the fundamental question is leadership. Who will have ultimate artistic authority – the team as a whole or one individual; what input and how much is to be expected from each person; if there is a dispute who has the final word and how will disputes be resolved; in the case of commissioned work will the promoter have the right to require changes?

Profit sharing

Prior collective agreement by collaborators as to the minimum and maximum hours of working and payment by way of set fee or a profit share scheme will also help avoid potential disputes.

A profit share scheme is where all the income derived from a performance is divided in previously agreed ratios after the deduction of certain expenses which might include hire costs for equipment – sound or lighting, etc, travel expenses and insurance. On a negative note, loss liability should also be discussed.

Once these points have been clarified and recorded, however informally, work can begin.

Ways out of a contract

The only way out of a contract is by its own terms – either by those stated or by those implied by law.

By performance

Where each party has completed his or her side of the bargain and nothing more remains to be done.

By agreement

The parties may decide to cancel the contract and mutually abandon their obligations.

By breach

Failure to complete through fault: in this situation the 'injured' party is entitled to claim damages or compensation for the loss caused by the breach. The object is to put the person not at fault in the same financial position had the contract been performed in its entirety. The contract may expressly provide what should be paid in the event of a breach through fault or, if litigation is necessary, the court will decide.

If there is a breach of a vital term the innocent person may treat the contract as at an end and sue for damages. For example a promoter engages an artist for two separate performances and agrees to pay a certain fee immediately after each. The promoter fails to pay after the first night in breach of the agreement. The artist is entitled to refuse to perform a second time and sue for damages for the loss sustained.

Failure to complete contract but through no fault: the contract may make provision for this and state that a person will not be in breach provided he/she has done all reasonably possible to complete his/her side of the contract. This might arise where due to unexpected traffic delays or extreme weather conditions the artist is unable to reach the venue to perform in time.

By frustration of contract

This occurs where, through no fault of either party, it becomes impossible to carry out the contract which automatically comes to an end. The contract would be frustrated if the venue was burnt down or the artist dies or is too ill to perform.

It is sensible to include in a contract terms covering cancellation and breach with details such as:

- Timescales in respect of the date of cancellation in relation to the performance date and percentage of fees payable on cancellation
- Which matters will allow the parties to be discharged from the contract, eg sickness, travel difficulties
- Insurance to cover cancellation
- Clauses linking payment to work done since the contract was agreed and before cancellation.

Contractual disputes

Often disputes are resolved by solutions significantly different from the strict legal position. The obvious reason for this is that insistence on legal rights might be disruptive to a continuing relationship between the parties and have a tendency to provide one or other with the reputation of being difficult to work with. Sometimes it is not possible to overcome the problem with the other person involved so what do you do – give up through lack of energy and time, obtain legal advice and/or issue court proceedings?

Legal advice

Free legal advice is available from Citizens Advice Bureaux (CAB) throughout the country and from solicitors operating Legal Aid schemes. To get Legal Aid you must see a solicitor. If you do not already have one ask your local CAB or Law Centre or a friend or relative for a recommendation. Consult the Solicitors' Regional Directory found in libraries and Law Centres which gives details of the kind of work solicitors' firms undertake. Whether you qualify for Legal Aid will depend on your savings and income and you may be required to contribute to legal costs.

In addition to the Legal Aid Scheme many solicitors are prepared to give up to half an hour's legal advice for £5. This is called a 'fixed fee interview' and is available regardless of your financial status. Solicitors' who provide this service are listed in the 'Solicitors' Regional Directory'.

Court proceedings

Contractual claims are heard in the County Court where less than £1000 is involved and for sums in excess of that, the High Court has jurisdiction unless it refers the matter to the County Court (as is increasingly the case for sums under £50,000). Magistrates and Crown Courts deal only with criminal matters.

Court procedure has been greatly simplified so it is possible to bring a 'small claim' (for sums under £1000) before the court without any knowledge of the law or legal representation. A useful booklet called 'Small Claims in the County Court' is issued by the Lord Chancellor's Department and is freely available from CAB.

Where more than £1000 is in dispute or if complicated issues need to be resolved it may be wise to take legal advice and get a solicitor to represent you. Litigation should be regarded as a last resort. It is expensive in terms of time, hassle and money if you are not legally aided and you should consider very carefully whether it is worth your while. There is no point in winning an action if your opponent is in no position to pay up.

Examples

The rest of this chapter has checklists for drawing up different types of contracts and licences.

Agreement appointing an agent

To: *(Name and address of Agent)*

Dear *(Agent's name)*,

This letter is to confirm that I have appointed you to act as my agent and you have agreed to act on my behalf. This agency shall be subject to the following terms:

1. Detail extent of Agent's duties:
   a. Arrange bookings and commissions for new work
   b. Arrange documentation
   c. Arrange publicity material, press coverage
   d. Arrange residencies, workshops, lectures
2. a. Is the Agency exclusive or can the artist appoint other agents?
   b. Is it to operate only in the UK, Europe, USA, worldwide?
   c. Can the Artist make independent arrangements?
   d. Does the Artist have the right to veto arrangements made by Agent?
3. How is the Agent to be paid? When and on what basis?
4. How is the Artist to be paid? When and on what basis?
5. How long is Agreement to last and is it renewable?
6. How can the Agreement be terminated and what notice is required?
7. How can the Agreement be altered in future?
8. Copyright – state that all copyright in the work remains the property of the artist and that the artist has asserted his/her moral right to be identified as the artist. What recording of the work is the agent allowed to do, for what purpose and who owns copyright in the recordings?

Please confirm your acceptance of the above by signing and returning the duplicate.

Signed *(Artist)*

Date

On the duplicate I agree and confirm the above.

Signed *(Agent)*

Date

Agreement between landowner and artist granting permission to perform

This should be used where a performance is to take place on private property but where the land owner is not a promoter and is merely providing a site.

To: *(Name and address of owner of land/premises)*,

This is to confirm that in consideration of the sum of £x paid by me to you on *(date)* (or if no payment is made then insert 'in consideration of the undertaking given by me and detailed below') you hereby grant me permission to perform outside the house/to enter the property known as (insert address) and perform there on (detail dates and times).

You acknowledge that I may perform without restriction and document any such performance and that the copyright therein belongs to me absolutely and that I have asserted my moral right to be identified as the artist.

If this undertaking is given then insurance cover is essential.

I undertake to make good or pay for any damage to your premises which may be caused by me. I also undertake to indemnify you against all legal liabilities in respect of claims by a third party resulting solely from a negligent act or omission on the part of my agents or representatives in the course of the performance on condition that you shall immediately notify me of any such claim.

Please confirm your acceptance of the above by signing and returning to me the duplicate copy of this letter.

Signed *(Artist)*
Date

On the duplicate

I agree and confirm the above.

Signed *(Landowner)*
Date

Agreement between promoter and artist booking an existing performance

Because of the diverse nature of live art it is impossible to draft one particular contract which will cover every situation. This is a basic contract with schedules which may be deleted, included or amended as appropriate.

Two copies of the Agreement should be issued with instructions that one copy should be completed where necessary, signed and returned within a certain number of days.

An Agreement made:

Date
Between Promoter *(name, address and telephone number)*
and Artist *(name, address and telephone number)*
for the performance of *(title of work)*
on *(date of performance)*
where *(venue)*

This agreement is subject to the specific schedules listed below which form an integral part of the Agreement.

1. Performance details
2. Financial arrangements
3. Technical facilities
4. Publicity arrangements
5. General conditions

Signed *(Promoter)*

Signed *(Artist)*

Schedule 1 **Performance details**

1. Title of work
2. Number of performances – dates, times, venue
3. Length of work – maximum and minimum duration, interval?
4. Age suitability
5. Restriction on performing elsewhere within certain radius for number of weeks?

Schedule 2 **Financial arrangements**

1. How is the fee to be calculated – guaranteed sum or box office split?
2. Is there a hire fee to be paid by the artist?
3. Is payment to be by cheque or in cash?
4. When is payment to be made – immediately after completion of performance? When will box office return be available?
5. Must the artist issue an invoice?
6. Ticket arrangements – price, concessions, to be fixed by whom? How many guest tickets will be issued?
7. Accommodation – is this required? For how many nights and how many people? Who will arrange it and who will pay?

Schedule 3 **Technical facilities**

1. Arrival and departure – dates and times
2. Access to space – dates, times and rehearsal availability. Size of performance area
3. Provision of entrances, exits and situation of audience
4. Refreshments – provided and paid for by whom?
5. Staffing availability – number, function and when?
6. Lighting, sound, tuned piano – who will provide what?
7. Is there a bar?
8. Parking availability

Schedule 4 **Publicity arrangements**

1. Detail what is required – leaflets, posters, size, quantity, over printing. Who is to bear cost, when must they be available?
2. Are photographs required and who will arrange and pay for them?
3. Who will prepare press releases if any?
4. What form will advertising take, who will undertake and pay for it – advertising in local/national press, direct mail?
5. Who will arrange printing of programmes and who will pay?
6. What control does the artist have over the form of advertising?

Schedule 5 **General conditions**

1. Insurance – what insurance cover does each party have? Are all requisite statutory and legal liabilities covered?

2. Licensing – does the promoter have the necessary licence to cover the performance, is a Performance Rights Society Licence required?
3. Copyright – state that all copyright in the work remains the property of the artist and that the artist has asserted his/her moral right to be identified as the artist. What recording of the work is the promoter allowed to do, for what purpose and who owns copyright in the recording?
4. Cancellation – what sums will be paid and at what stage – prior to performance and during? How will the fees be calculated – lump sum or based on anticipated ticket sales? What eventualities will allow the parties to cancel without penalty?

Contract commissioning new work

An Agreement made:

Date

Between Promoter *(name, address, telephone number)*

and Artist *(name, address, telephone number)*

To commission a new work entitled *(title of work)*

This Agreement is subject to the specific schedules listed below which form an integral part of the Agreement.

1. Performance details
2. The context
3. Payment arrangements
4. Publicity
5. Documentation
6. General conditions

Signed *(Promoter)*

Signed *(Artist)*

Schedule 1 Performance details

1. Brief description of the work
2. Length of piece
3. When is it to be performed and how many times?
4. May artist alter work from that described?
5. May promoter require changes in work?

Schedule 2 The context

1. Is a site provided, of what nature? Where is it? How accessible is it? During what hours, how far in advance and in what circumstances?
2. Is a studio or workplace provided and details thereof?
3. Is accommodation provided – where is it, who should arrange and pay for it?
4. Is equipment provided and at whose expense?
5. Is technical support available – lighting, sound?
6. Is catering provided – at whose expense?

Schedule 3 Payment arrangements

1. How much – fixed sum or related to box office receipts or a combination?
2. What does it cover – are expenses included or additional?
3. When is the fee to be paid – cheque or cash?

Schedule 4 Publicity arrangements

1. Detail what is required – leaflets, posters, size, quantity, over printing – who is to bear cost, when must they be available?
2. Are photographs required and who will arrange and pay for them?
3. Who will prepare press releases if any?
4. What form will advertising take, who will undertake and pay for it – advertising in local/national press, direct mail?
5. Who will arrange printing of programmes and who will pay?
6. What control does the artist/promoter have over the form of advertising?

Schedule 5 Documentation

1. What form will it take?
2. Who organises and pays for it?
3. Does artist/promoter have control over its ultimate form?
4. Who retains the documentation and who owns the copyright to it?

Schedule 6 General Conditions

1. Insurance – what insurance cover does each party have? Are all requisite statutory and legal liabilities covered?
2. Cancellation – what sums will be paid and at what stage – prior to performance and during? How will the fees be calculated –

lump sum or based on anticipated ticket sales? What eventualities will allow the parties to cancel without penalty?

3. Copyright – state that all copyright in the work remains the property of the artist and that the artist has asserted his/her moral right to be identified as the artist.

Licence to another to perform a work

To be used when an artist grants to another person or licensee the right to perform the artist's work. This may be alien and offensive to those who consider their work to be entirely personal but for an established live artist it might provide a useful source of income

Name and address of artist

Name and address of licensee

1. Details of work to be licensed – title and brief description, date created and author/s. What documentation will be given to the licensee and when will it be returned?
2. Is licence to be exclusive or may artist grant similar licence to another? Is licence restricted to UK, USA, Europe, worldwide? May artist perform the work him/herself during term of licence?
3. Length of licence, is it renewable and how may it be cancelled?
4. What credit will the artist be given as the author in all publicity and advertising material relating to the work – what control does the artist have over this material?
5. Does the licensee have any right to edit or alter the work? May the artist cancel the licence if the quality of the licensee's performance is unacceptable?
6. Does the Agreement specify how many times the licensee must perform the work?
7. Payment – how is the artist to be paid? A Royalty by way of a percentage of box office receipts for each performance, a set sum or a combination? When is the artist to be paid?
8. Copyright – ensure that all copyright in the work remains the property of the artist and that you have asserted the moral right to be identified as the artist. State that nothing in the licence amounts to an assignment or transfer of copyright to the licensee.

Signed *(Artist)*

Signed *(Licensee)*

Date

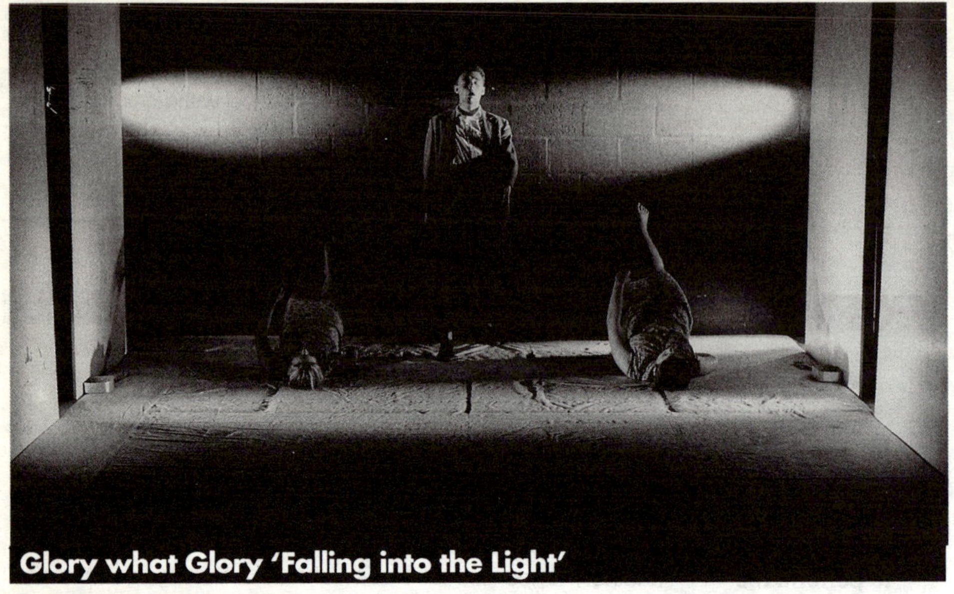

Glory what Glory 'Falling into the Light'

Our work combines elements of text, choreography and arresting visuals (through set design and lighting). For this reason, although the majority of the company trained in theatre studies, we cannot and will not ignore the value of the other disciplines.

In our first year we were in receipt of Enterprise Allowance (£40 per week each). With an initial investment of £1000 in the bank, our aim was to break even. We did, but only just. The second show was far trickier – book-keeping and budgeting was/is a nightmare. We survived on a personal level by signing on or doing stints of temporary work to make ends meet. I think we all felt that if our claim for Arts Council funding for the third show was unsuccessful we would seriously have to reconsider the viability of the future of the company. Fortunately it didn't come to that. Now we are in receipt of funding and can at last afford to pay ourselves wages – what luxury! I find it difficult to imagine how we could continue as a company if we were not funded for our next show or any show beyond.

We are constantly searching for the 'best' way of selling our work to venues. Still the answer eludes us! Sending brief, honest details about the company and previous work and the show in question is how we went about programming the tour for 'Inertia Real'. We also make available (upon request) a short promotional video containing extracts from our last two shows. We find this very useful to demonstrate the important visual and physical aspects of our work, which are inevitably difficult to describe accurately on paper.

17 • Copyright

by David Butler

Because live art crosses the boundaries of other artforms copyright can be quite complex. Neither live art nor performance art are considered specific categories of work by the 1988 copyright act. Separate elements of a live work may be treated as separate copyright works – sculpture, sound recording, musical work, film. Also all, or part, of the performance itself may, depending on its content and form, be treated for copyright purposes as a 'dramatic work' (this same description protects plays, dance and mime) – providing it has been recorded in tangible form. This last requirement is often problematic for live art . The copyright act also gives a new separate form of protection for live performances – performing rights. The copyright in the live work itself, or elements of it, is quite separate from the copyright in the recording of that work. AN Publications book 'Artists handbook 4: Copyright', by Roland Miller, looks at copyright in detail (what is copyright, who owns it, how to use it, writing a licence or contract, reproduction fees, royalties, moral rights, infringements, using solicitors, copyright abroad, etc). This chapter gives a brief overview of copyright relating to live art. It only deals with the 1988 copyright act which generally applies to works created after 1 August 1989.

see 21 • Further reading

The uses of copyright

A copyright work can generally only be 'copied' with the permission of the copyright owner – usually the artist. This gives the artist the power to stop others infringing the artist's copyright. It also gives the artist the chance to make money by charging others for the right to reproduce the artist's work.

'Copying' means different things depending on the nature of the work. For an artistic work (eg a sculpture or painting) it includes copying a two-dimensional work in three dimensions and vice versa. For dramatic, musical and literary works, it includes performing, showing or playing the work in public. In every case it also includes issuing copies to the public. A 'substantial part' of a copyright work must be copied before there is infringement, but this can physically be a very small part if it is an essential part.

Dramatic, literary and musical works must be recorded in some way before they are capable of copyright protection. Recording could be, for instance, filming the entire work. A written script would also be classed as a recording – provided it would allow someone else to perform the work and is sufficiently detailed. Performance of the work is not itself sufficient to give copyright protection.

see 16 • Contracts

The right to copy belongs exclusively to the artist. You can give someone permission (a licence) to copy work and you can charge them a fee for this. If you are permitting someone to copy work do so in writing, even if this is just a letter, making it clear what can be copied, where, when, for how long, in what form, for what fee. For example you might agree with a postcard company that they can reproduce an image from a particular performance, crediting title of work and you as artist, as a postcard, in a print run of 5000, for distribution in the UK over the next two years, at an agreed fee or royalty, with an option to print more at a fee or royalty to be renegotiated. You should never agree to 'assign' your copyright. This means you are giving it away for good.

Infringements

If your copyright has been infringed, you can take civil proceedings (in the County or High Court) to stop this or to obtain damages. The infringer may also be committing a criminal offence. However legal action is often uncertain and could be expensive. You should first deal directly with the infringer and try to get them to destroy, or remove from circulation, the copies. Or you might want to agree payment with them in return for you agreeing to take no action. But be clear what they are paying for. Don't make an agreement which implies they can just go on making copies. If a direct approach fails you should take professional advice. Free legal advice is available from Citizens' Advice Bureaux. The solicitor at an advice centre will not normally be a copyright specialist and can't act for you but it is a useful first port of call, and they may be able to refer you to a local solicitor.

Exceptions

There are exceptions to copyright protection. Three of these are known as fair dealing and permit copying for:

- Research or private study
- Criticism or review (eg in a magazine)
- Reporting of current events (eg in a newspaper or on TV). This is very broad and could enable your work to be filmed or videoed, and broadcast without any acknowledgement or permission.

There is another exception to the effect that there is no infringement where a work is 'incidentally' included in an artistic work, sound recording, film, broadcast or cable transmission.

Protecting the work

Much live art, of course, simply 'happens'. The work begins, ends and that's it. So if someone photographs the work, turns the photograph into a postcard and sells it how do you show they have infringed your copyright?

If you are using 'props', such as sculptures, paintings, drawings, or film, video or photographs, these may be separately protected as distinct copyright works and therefore be protected against unauthorised reproduction, unless any of the above exceptions apply. But other elements of a live work will only attract protection as a dramatic work if they are recorded in tangible form (eg in writing or by a film, video or photograph). The recording will constitute proof the work existed and can be used as evidence against infringers.

You can also achieve some protection against unauthorised filming or photographs by including a written statement on tickets and programmes that admission is conditional on there being no unauthorised reproduction of any part of the work. This should enable you to take legal action for breach of contract.

For many live artists recording a work is problematic. For example documentation becomes another work, live action is improvised, ownership of a work is 'given away' by performing it, etc. So copyright protection can be an ethical dilemma and in the end you can only sort this out for yourself.

see • 13 Documentation

Documentation

Having someone photograph or video your work is one occasion when copyright becomes an issue. Who owns the copyright on a photograph, film or video?

With photographs it is the photographer who automatically owns the copyright. With film or video the copyright belongs to the person who arranges for the film or video to be made. If you commission someone to film a performance, tell them what you want and pay them, you are effectively the film producer and the copyright belongs to you. But these rules are uncertain and it is much better to have a clear agreement covering the issues.

In all cases what is important is for the artist and photographer/film maker to agree what each can do with the photograph, film or video. You may want a set of photographs to form an archive, use for publicity, make a postcard from, use in another work. The photographer may want to exhibit the photograph, sell it to a magazine, use it for their own publicity. As long as you are both clear and in agreement about these permitted uses there should be no problem. But once you have agreed, write it down and make sure when the photographer uses the photograph they credit both you as artist and the title of the work. Likewise you should credit the photographer. Label any copy (photograph, postcard, video, etc) with title of the work, © symbol, your name, and the date the work was made.

If you make an agreement it will save you arguing later about the intricacies of copyright. Ask yourself – what do I want to use this photograph or video for and what do I not want it used for? Get the photographer/film maker to ask the same question and sort out any differences between these viewpoints before you agree to go ahead.

see 16 • Contracts

You should bear all this in mind when signing any contract with a promoter, commissioner, venue, etc. Copyright is often not mentioned in contracts. It should be and it can be sorted out simply. Both the promoter and the artist each have legitimate reasons for recording a live art event. Sort out what each wants to do and write it down.

Moral rights

Moral rights give you the right to:

- Be acknowledged as the artist (right of authorship or paternity). This has to be asserted in writing in all contracts with third parties (eg the venue where the work is appearing) and any licence agreements. Use a statement such as 'The right of (name of artist) to be identified as author of (identify work) has been asserted generally in accordance with sections 77 and 78 of the Copyright, Designs and Patents Act 1988'. But even where the right has been asserted there are complex rules about who is and who is not bound by your rights.

- Object to 'derogatory treatment' of work (right of integrity) – eg a 'scratch' video being made from your work.
- Not be wrongly identified as author of a work (right to prevent false attribution)
- Not to have privately commissioned photographs, films or videos (eg of a wedding) misused by others (right of privacy).

Copyright ownership and length of protection

The duration of copyright protection differs from work to work. The following list is not comprehensive.

- Artistic works (sculpture, painting, printmaking, drawing, photography, craft) – copyright belongs to the artist and lasts for the artist's life plus 50 years.
- Film, video and sound recording – copyright belongs to the *'person by whom the arrangements necessary for the making of the film* (or sound recording) *are made'* and lasts for 50 years after the film/ video or sound recording was made or released.
- Musical work – copyright belongs to the composer and lasts for the artist's life plus 50 years.
- Literary works – copyright belongs to the author and lasts for the artist's life plus 50 years.
- Dramatic works – copyright belongs to the author and lasts for the artist's life plus 50 years.

Performing rights

Performing rights relate to performers and people owning recording rights to a performance. A recording means a film or sound recording made directly from the performance, or from a broadcast, or from another recording of the performance. You own the recording rights on your own live art work provided it is a qualifying 'performance' under the act. You can license these to other people just as with copyright. A qualifying performance would be:

- A dramatic performance (including dance and mime)
- A musical performance
- A reading or recital of a literary work
- A variety act or any similar presentation

You own the rights to your performance in any live art work, even if it is not a piece of your devising. This also means that if you use other artists in a live art work of your devising they own the rights on their 'performance'. So if you are recording a performance your contract with the other performers should include an agreement to you using the recording, stating clearly what it can be used for, where, when, how, etc. You may agree you can use a video of a work for your publicity, for showing privately, as part of an exhibition; but not agree that it can be broadcast on national TV without prior agreement, or payment of an additional fee.

Like copyright, you can take action against someone infringing your performing rights, for example by distributing illicit recordings. The permitted acts relating to copyright broadly relate to performing rights.

Performing and recording rights last for 50 years after the performance takes place.

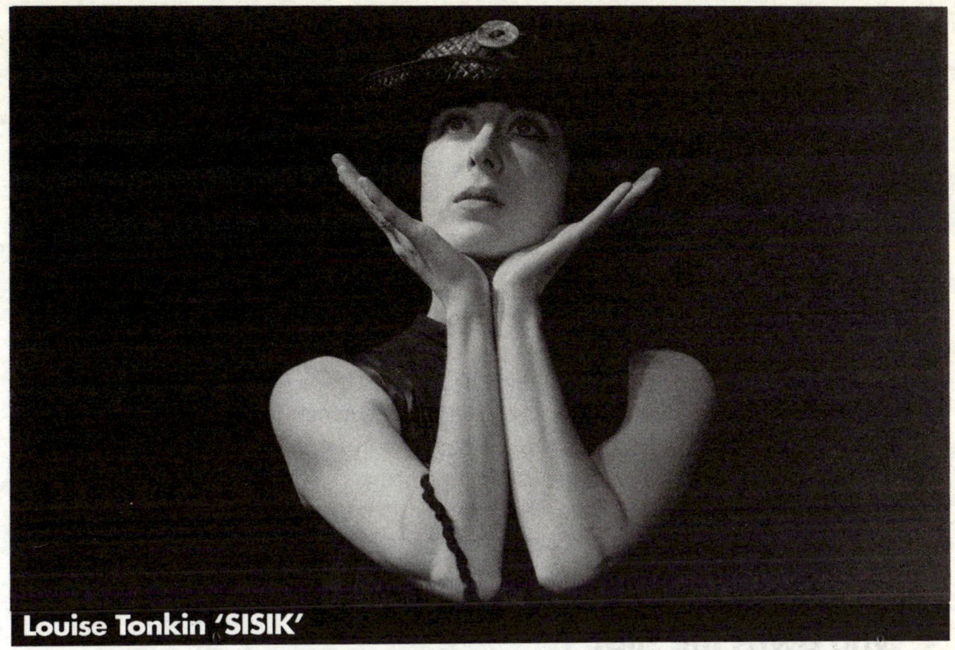

Louise Tonkin 'SISIK'

I started working in live art when Kettle's Yard, Cambridge invited me to perform my dance theatre show SISIK. As part of an exhibition 'Revolutions 1789-1989', I was asked to direct a performance with this as its theme. The resulting questioning open-ended performance has, with other influences, led my work to a live art form.

I work with sculptor Phyllida Barlow. We recently completed another residency at Kettle's Yard, finding possibilities of changing space with form using the human body, lengths of hardboard and stepladders.

I have expected audiences and venue managers to be very 'literal' in their desire to see and perceive an event, but I've been pleasantly surprised by openness and desire to accept. This is not always true, and as my work progresses I expect more 'opaque' faces – I may be wrong. My belief is if the intention is honest and clear and the means of expression effective and exciting, then an audience will glean that, even if at times they may find the whole baffling.

So publicising work can be difficult – avoiding the wilfully obscure, or the overliteral 'niceties'. My current publicity tends to paint everything with the same brush and be over wordy. So I may lose out on the very venues where I'd like to perform and obtain the more acceptable. Juggling with funds, precludes following every publicity mailout with a phone call. Too often material just sits on a promoter's desk. Response is either 'very interested' or 'not at all'. Live art is a minority interest, but I feel promoters and venues can nurture this sentiment at the cost of accessibility.

Photo: Gary Burgess

18 • Legal permissions

by Bush Hartshorn

Imagine: you've found this fantastic place – your vision of what could happen is burning a hole in you and somehow you've managed to get some money to help you do it. But this is Britain in the '90s, and people can be very nervous of public gatherings, the new and innovative, the abnormal – the characteristic encapsulated by 'live art'. So tread carefully, your 'people management' is the key to your success.

Who owns the site?

This can obviously vary hugely; private, state, council, church. Probably the best way is to ask around the vicinity, the corner shop, etc. Once you've found the owner you can identify the decision maker. If the property is for sale then negotiations will have to be via the estate agent. Decisions about council property may have to be agreed by committee or with private property you may be dealing with a jovial farmer with ruddy cheeks. Each decision maker will require their own individually tailored approach.

But whoever the decision maker is, I have always described what I would like to do in terms that are readily understandable. For example, I would call an installation an exhibition, a performance, a play. Be prepared for the question *'what's it all about'*. Most questions will concern how many people will be coming, when you will want to be there, whether you have insurance, what are the security arrangements?

see 16 • Contracts

Remember the person giving you permission wants to have confidence that you're not going to incite a riot, burn the place down, hold an acid house party. But one word of advice – don't lie too much.

After successful performances by Industrial and Domestic Theatre Contractors (the company I work with) I have asked the person giving permission to write a testimonial to be used on other occasions to nudge those more reluctant to relent. So after careful and sometimes long-winded negotiation they give permission – you should then draw up an agreement and get it signed. Always keep a copy with you whenever you are on site to show to any passing inquirer such as the local constabulary.

When you do finally move on to it, remember you are *borrowing* the site and any complaints about noise and rubbish will go straight to the land owner who probably won't want that kind of attention. So cultivate your neighbours, inform them of what you're doing and keep sound and pyrotechnic testing to reasonable times of day. The offer of a free ticket always goes down well. Now comes the complicated bit.

How do you get a licence?

The licence you want is an 'Occasional Theatre Licence' and possibly a 'Public Entertainment Licence'. These are issued by the local authority environmental health department licensing division, who can tell you whether they apply to your event. If they do you will need four sets of your application: one for the environmental health department, one for the fire brigade, one for the police and one for yourself. The fire and police will send back their observations to the environmental health officer. You are about to embark upon a relationship with the environmental health officer and they are almost inevitably men in suits. But beware of stereotyping. Some of these local authority officers have very lively minds and will enjoy helping you achieve your vision.

Fire and safety regulations should always be obeyed without question – think of the Dublin and New York Disco fires, the Isle of Man leisure centre fire, Kings Cross, Hillsborough, etc. I see no point in any artform endangering life.
Roland Miller

Before your first appointment with this person you should be as clear as possible about what you want to do. Bear in mind the environmental health officer is paid to protect the interests of the public, so they are primarily looking at the safety aspects followed by the inconvenience to the public. But they are not interested in stopping you from doing something. Their job is to help you put on the event while protecting the public interest.

When you first meet it should ideally be on site and you should be accompanied by the person from your side who will be responsible for the technical aspects of your work: lights, sound, etc. I have found the best approach is to seek the environmental health office's advice about the things they would want doing before they grant a licence.

The environmental health office will want to know numbers of people expected to attend; the audience's points of entry; your ushering arrangements (I have found a great deal can be made possible by having well-trained ushers with torches); whether the audience will be seated or standing. The environmental health office in consultation with the fire officer will give you your audience capacity. This is primarily related to the means of escape, how many doors, how quickly and efficiently the building can be evacuated. You may have a building which can hold twenty thousand people but if you can only get two thousand out in the required time, this will be licensed capacity. As a general rule the fire officer usually applies a formula of one hundred people per single door width (700mm).

The fire officer is now becoming an important part of your team and you will need their advice. You need to make your request for advice to the county fire officer at headquarters, pointing out where the event will take place. It will then get routed to the appropriate Fire Safety Officer who will contact you. The fire officer will consult their Bible, the 'Guide to fire precautions in existing places of entertainment and like premises' (Home Office, 1990, HMSO, £8.50 – available in large libraries and from HMSO Bookshops. Not what I would recommend as a good read but it has all the information you will need.

Performances have been restricted, mainly here in UK, by safety and fire regulations, I have always tried to work around these situations, talking over the problems, etc, making sure no one will get injured or hurt. Infact it is usually myself who has been injured, being hospitalised twice on different occaisions with eye injuries, there are many instances where I have been injured, too many maybe, but this is not through incompetence.
Andre Stitt

You will find you have to have:

- Minimum of a five foot unobstructed width to all fire exits
- Emergency fire exits clearly signed
- Emergency lighting system with battery back up (these can be hired, if you are using generators the emergency lighting must be powered by a separate generator to the main lighting)
- Sufficient ushers (I suggest one per hundred audience with a torch)
- A fire drill procedure and the people to carry it out.

Fire officers are very strict about fire exits, so keep them clear at all times. If you have cable runs going across them ensure they are taped down and the audience won't trip over them. Otherwise fly them over the exit.

You will also need fire extinguishers:

- Water (red) for general purpose
- CO_2 (black) for electrical
- Dry Powder (blue) for catering operations.

These can also be hired and the fire officer will advise you on the appropriate number and their positioning.

Scenery and props will also be inspected. The fire officer walks up to your set, gets a cigarette lighter, ignites it and holds it under your set for anything up to thirty seconds. They do not want it to catch light, it must self extinguish. You may treat cloth and paper with brand name fire retardants such as 'Flambar' – if you want to keep, wear or reuse things then this is recommended. Otherwise try my Mrs Beeton recipe which is much cheaper but you should test the items carefully with a cigarette lighter. There are three types. For all of them I always warm the water first, then add the chemicals. Soak the items in the solution and allow to drain. Do not rinse. Non of these are recommended for clothing.

- Coarse fabrics and scenery:
  - Boracic acid 9lbs/4kilos
  - Sodium phosphate 6lbs/2.75kilos
  - Water 10 gals / 46 litres
- Delicate fabrics and cotton wool:
  - Borax 10oz/300gms
  - Boracic acid 8oz/240gms
  - Water 1 gal / 4.6 litres
- Domestic material:
  - Borax 7oz/200gms
  - Boracic acid 3oz/85gms
  - Water 4 pints / 2.25 litres

If there is to be no smoking then put up the relevant signs. If smoking is allowed provide ashtrays. Smoking on stage usually requires sand or water in an ashtray.

I think it is important to stress that fire officers, after giving their advice, will inspect and may not announce their inspection. But they are reasonable people and a mature and caring approach may well convince them to let you do extraordinary things. Industrial and Domestic once did a performance in a church lit entirely by candles – up to five hundred burning at one time. Ushers with extinguishers were standing by.

There is always some danger lurking in effective art, but it should be from upsetting prejudice and confronting bigotry, ie the danger of revolutionary ideas, not from actual physical harm. I would always stop a performance if I saw real physical danger to spectators.
Roland Miller

Don't be lulled into a false sense of security because your performance is outside and there is nothing to catch fire, still get the Fire Officer to inspect for your own peace of mind.

Meanwhile you and the environmental health office are getting along just fine and you have begun to look closer at the site. All manner of things may crop up.

In 1983, Nikki Millican of the Midland Group, Nottingham commissioned Industrial and Domestic to perform in a disused swimming pool. At the first site meeting the environmental health officer discovered blue asbestos in the building. He asked us to seal it behind a film of polythene and said he would come and do an air test to ascertain whether the air contained dangerous levels of asbestos. The test on Monday failed but by Thursday the level had dropped sufficiently and we were issued with a licence.

A lot of problems you may encounter are surmountable given the right approach.

If you are using seats it is preferable for them to be fixed to whatever structure they are placed upon. But they must be fastened together (gaffer tape will suffice but cable ties are better). This is to prevent chairs scattering everywhere and becoming entangled in people's legs in the panic which may ensue during an emergency exit. The Environmental Health Officer will tell you how many seats you can have before an aisle and the width of the aisle (usually three feet).

You may want to hang things from the ceiling or drive forklifts across the floor. Enter the structural engineer usually from the building department or the same local authority as your environmental health officer. The structural engineer will want weight information to do their calculations on loadings. If your performance has a space beneath it this may also have an effect on the audience numbers. These numbers can also be restricted by toilet facilities (which can be hired – Portaloo) and parking and access for emergency vehicles. This is an area which the police will be interested in, so early consultation with them is also advised. Address your request for advice to the Chief Superintendent of the division within which the event will take place. You can get this information from your local police station.

If you are using scaffolding in any quantity it is probably best to get someone with a scaffolding certificate to erect it, although this can be got around by using the Cuplock system. If this is the case you may well be welcoming a new member of the team from the same local authority – the planning department. Some temporary structures such as tents or even scaffolding pyramids may require planning permission. Structural changes and altered use are two other areas where the planning department may get involved. But by now you and the Environmental Health Officer are getting on so well there should be no problems!

You should now be in a position to start drawing scale plans so site visits are less necessary and discussions can take place in the office.

There are always fire and safety restrictions and so I either comply or ignore the rules depending on the nature of the work. The police have been called to sites where I have been working. When 'The State Welfare Project' was located in Reading, police arrived after compliants had been lodged. I had been breaking a number of milk bottles within the outdoor installation. The element of discussion within the work meant that any debate with the police was incorporated within the form of the project.

Tim Brennan

At that first site visit with your technician, the environmental health officer will have enquired about the electrical aspects of your production. I have already covered emergency lighting and must confess to being a little 'electrophobic', but always enjoy the enthusiasm of the technicians and the environmental health officer talking about earthing spikes and various phrases.

Essentially the environmental health officer will look at provision and distribution of supply. Most electrical equipment will need to be an arm's reach or five feet from the audience.

Any metal work such as scaffolding, seating unit, will have to be earth bonded, that is you purchase an earth bond, strap it to the metal and attach it to a ground, such as a copper cold water pipe (always check with an electrician). If you are outdoors you do the same thing but with an earthing spike.

The other thing to be aware of is noise pollution, this is also dealt with by your environmental health officer who will advise you on local decibel levels. This is a highly emotive area, with fear of rock concerts, acid house parties, etc. The police may well have objections so again early consultation is advised. Once you have permission be wary of turning up the volume, there may well be an environmental health officer with a decibel meter ready to swoop in and turn you off.

Other considerations

So finally you have permission from the landowner, you have an 'Occasional Theatre Licence', now get some insurance. The type of insurance you want is 'public liability' with an indemnity of a minimum of one million pounds. The best way to get this is to go to a registered broker. (AN Publications 'Fact Pack 6: Insurance' will give you details of different types of insurance.) The British Insurance and Investment Brokers Association (BIIBA) will supply you with information about your area. British Insurance and Investment Brokers Association, BIIBA House, 14 Bevis House, London EC3A 7NT. Telephone 071 623 9043.

You may feel more at ease if you have qualified first aiders on site. St John's Ambulance are very willing to provide this service. They require at least six week's notice and make a small charge depending on how many people you require and whether, for example, you need an ambulance to be present.

Should you want to signpost your event the RAC and the AA will help you put up those little signs but you need permission from the engineers department of your local authority. Should you want the lights disconnecting for a blackout then see the highways department.

How long will this all take?

For a problem-free application with nothing too extraordinary I would allow an absolute minimum of three months. Negotiate the date for the first inspection and allow yourself time to put things right before the actual event remembering they will want to inspect again before giving the licence. If the application is likely to be more problematic make your first approaches nine to twelve months in advance. Remember these licences are only a small part of the environmental health departments work.

Finally, I hope this chapter is a useful introduction to a process which can be time consuming, frustrating and at times confusing, dealing with people who can be completely opposed to many views that we artists hold. I can only stress again the importance of the relationship between you or your representative and the various authorities to be dealt with. I was once advised to approach each meeting as if I was going to court (interpret that as you like). I have found it to be good advice.

May I take this opportunity to make a plea. When your event is over please return the space to the owner as you found it with any damage made good. Another artist may want to use the space or the owner may own other good spaces – this will make getting permissions easier for all of us. One bad apple can ruin the basket.

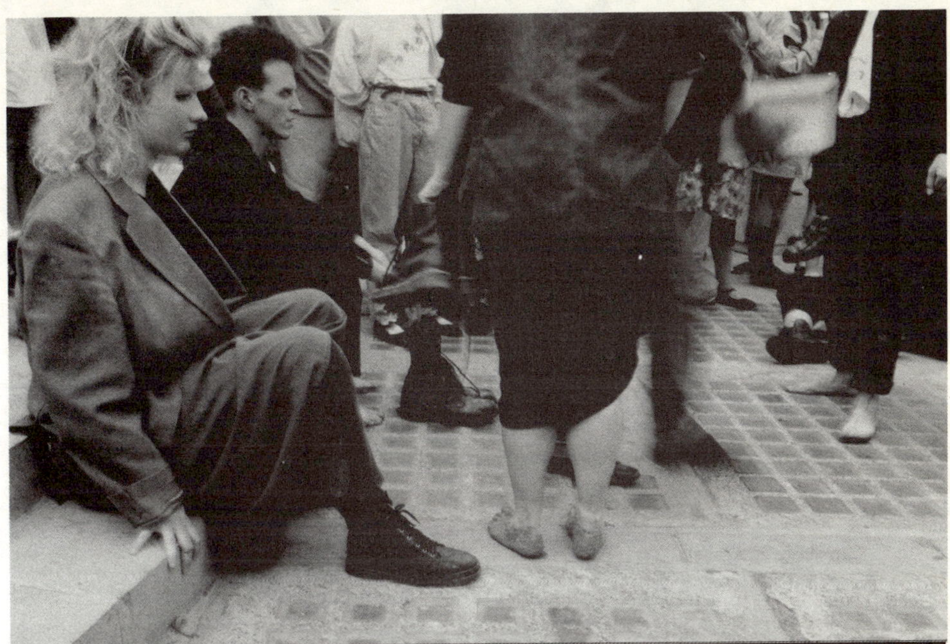

Mike Stubbs, Hull Time Based Arts

If performances are presented in pedestrianised precincts never underestimate audience size, emotional response, and provide stewardship for crowd control. Hull Time Based Arts got caught out when we commissioned Man Act to produce 'Monument' as part of Hull Festival; the theme of the festival was the French Revolution. A Saturday afternoon in the city centre produced an audience of between 1000 and 1500 people. The performance had been devised through a week's 'physical theatre' workshop with 15 local performers of mixed experience who took part in the final presentation. Imagine their surprise as the crowd got closer and closer, blocking the path of a run and rock smash. The three stewards could not cope with the sheer quantity of people pushing and shoving to see what was happening. In addition to this the Mayor of Hull who had been dragged out of the City Hall by a photographer from the Hull Daily Mail, to be set up for a photograph examining supposed 'damaged paving stones' done by the performers, used the situation as a platform to present a highly entertaining performance which involved removing his chain, getting threatening and making an impromptu speech on vandalism.

The lessons are:

- watch the press
- have enough stewards/don't underestimate audience turnout
- have full insurance cover
- inform the relevant authorities (council/police) of as much detail as possible.

The photograph shows 'Monument' by Man Act, with local performers in Hull.

19 • Legal constraints

by Juliet Burgess

It should come as no surprise that art that seeks to challenge preconception should sometimes meet with attempt to repress. This chapter gives a brief overview of some legislation that can be used to prevent, censor or control live artists.

Obscenity

This topic is relevant in so far as the artist may possess and distribute what is considered 'obscene' advertising material, own 'obscene' documentation of a performance or perform an 'obscene' work. Prosecutions for obscenity are increasingly rare these days but promoters may be wary and often issue contracts with editorial control over material in order to keep within the relevant statutes. For instance in one case the word 'fuck' was voluntarily removed from a live artist's publicity posters in order to appease the promoters.

Obscene Publications Acts 1959 &1964

These Acts provide that a person who publishes, whether for gain or not, an obscene article is guilty of a criminal offence punishable with a maximum of three years' imprisonment.

What is an article?
This is defined as anything containing matter to be read or looked at or both, any sound record, any film or other record of a picture or pictures. This includes photographs, negatives and videos, and would cover publicity material for a performance and documentation.

What is publishing?
This means distributing, circulating, selling, lending, giving, hiring, offering for sale or hire and in the case of a film or video, showing, playing or projecting it.

What is obscene?

An article is deemed obscene if its effect taken as a whole is such as to tend to deprave and corrupt persons who are likely, having regard to all the circumstances, to read, see or hear the matter contained in it. Obscenity is not confined to sex. It can cover material likely to induce violence or drug taking. In 1985 there was a successful prosecution against a publication on cocaine entitled 'Attention Coke Lovers. Free Base. The Greatest Thing Since Sex' (R v Skirving 1985 2 AER 705).

The legal meaning given to 'obscene' is very specialised and difficult to define in general terms. In practice it will vary from jury to jury as it is they who ultimately decide what is likely to deprave and corrupt.

Defences

A defence is available if the accused can show they had not examined the article in question and had no reasonable cause to suspect it was obscene.

A further defence is if it can be shown the publication was for the public good on the ground it was in the interests of science, literature or other objects of general concern. In the case of a moving picture film or soundtrack this is extended to being in the interests of drama, opera, ballet or any other art or learning.

I think censorship can be circumvented with subtlety, or turned on itself by exposure – you have to be careful, however. Actually opposing censorship is a legitimate role for live art. One of the great virtues of the form (and another argument against touring fixed, known product) is its ability to change and alter, thus avoiding censorship.
Roland Miller

Possession of an obscene article

It is an offence to have an obscene article for publication for gain, whether this is gain for oneself or another person. A person is deemed to have committed this offence if with a view to publication, as defined above, that person has the article in his or her ownership, possession or control.

Forfeiture

Obscene articles kept on premises for publication for gain may be seized under a search warrant issued by a magistrate. The defence of public good is again available in proceedings of this kind.

Theatres Act 1968

This Act prohibits the presentation of obscene performances of plays whether given in public or private.

What is obscene?

The test is as before, namely it is deemed obscene if its effect, taken as a whole, has a tendency to deprave or corrupt persons who, having regard to all the relevant circumstances, were likely to attend it.

Who is liable?

Any person who presents or directs an obscene performance is criminally liable and punishable with a fine or up to three years' imprisonment. The offence is not committed merely by virtue of performing but if a performer had helped develop the work in addition then that artist would be liable.

What is a play?

This is interpreted as any dramatic piece whether involving improvisation or not which is given wholly or in part by one or more persons actually present and performing, in which the major proportion of what is done by the persons performing whether by speech singing or action involves the playing of a role. A court would have little difficulty in including most live art displays within this definition.

Powers of entry and inspection

A magistrate may issue a warrant if there are reasonable grounds for suspecting an infringement of the Act thereby allowing police to enter premises to inspect and to attend a performance.

What defences are available?

There cannot be a proper prosecution if the performance is a rehearsal or given in a private dwelling on a domestic occasion or to enable a record or broadcast to be made. Otherwise the defence of public good can be used as before.

Local Government Act 1988

by David Butler

Local authorities are important in the funding and support of art. So artists can fall foul of the Local Government Act 1988, which controls the functions and statutory obligations of local authorities. This legislation can only be invoked against a local authority not against an artist or a promoter. But it can be used as a reason to remove funding, premises, etc, or through the threat of such action, to censor an event.

Sections 2 & 4

These prevent a local authority from publishing *'any material which, in whole or part, appears to be designed to affect public support for a political party'*. In 1989 this was used by Southwark Council to remove references to socialism and Margaret Thatcher from the catalogue of the exhibition 'Ireland the Right to Know'. The film and video programme with the exhibition was 'deferred'.

Section 28

This prevents a local authority from intentionally promoting homosexuality, publishing material with the intention of promoting homosexuality, or promoting the teaching in a school of the acceptability of homosexuality as a *'pretended family relationship'.*

'We 2 Girls Together Clinging' was created pre-section 28. One promoter did not want to take the risk when the legislation first appeared. As an artist I do feel far more vulnerable although I am determined not to self censor.
Nenagh Watson

A Department of the Environment circular of December 1988 states that, *'so long as [authorities] are not setting out to promote homosexuality they may... fund theatre and other arts events which may include homosexual themes'.* Richard Luce, when minister for the arts, stated in a letter to the Association of Metropolitan Authorities, *'If, for example, an authority clearly had a policy of seeking to bring the work of all sorts of artists and playwrights before the public and from time to time put on exhibitions or plays for this purpose, the fact that the artists concerned include some who were homosexual would not put the local authority at risk under the section. The local authority's intention would clearly be the promotion of art rather than the promotion of homosexuality'.*

Government circulars and letters do not have the force of law but are important guides to how the government feels law should be interpreted.

Challenging the law

Section 28 has never been tested in the courts. It is a weapon of fear and self-censorship that has been foisted onto local government legislation (as are sections 2 and 4). It is invoked because of prejudice or fear of criticism. The law being used to support prejudice is nothing new. Artwork dealing with gay and lesbian sexuality, for instance, suffers more from charges of obscenity than heterosexual artwork. Fear of criticism depends on lack of knowledge of the law. This can and should be challenged. 'Section 28, a practical guide to the law and its implications', published by Liberty, gives a detailed background to section 28 and outlines legal challenges. A number of these rest on the fact that local authorities have legal responsibilities that can override section 28. This can also apply to other abuses of the local government act.

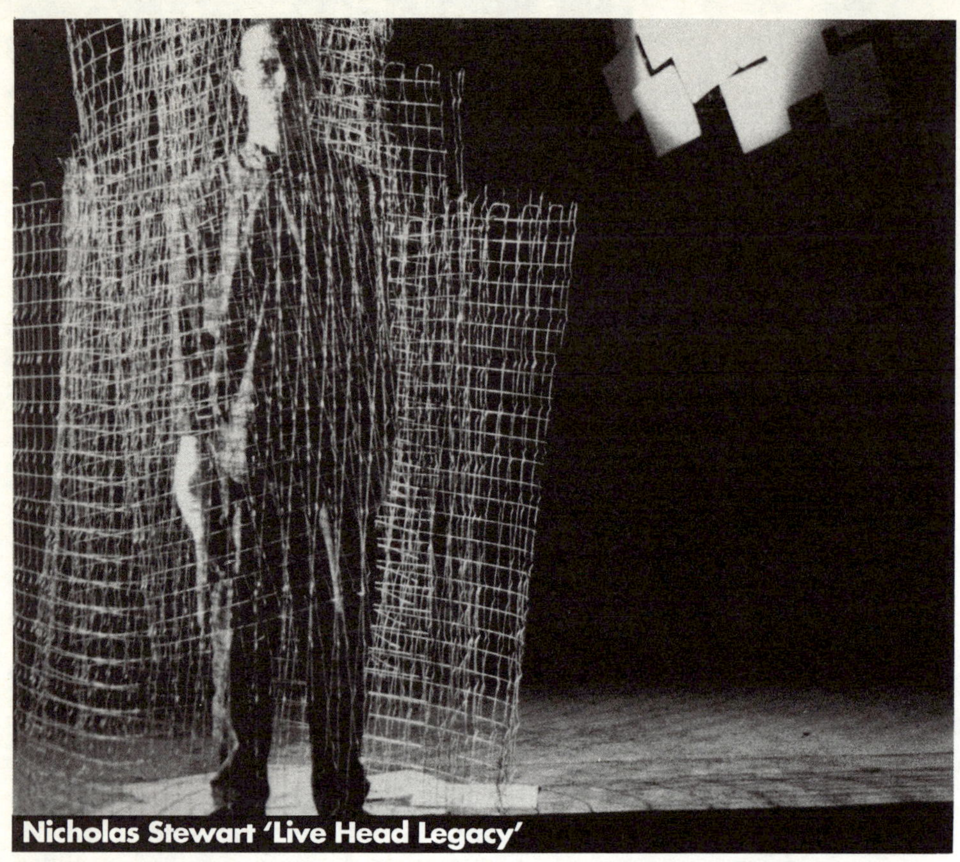

Nicholas Stewart 'Live Head Legacy'

I have never seen the term live art as an exclusive definitive category. Rather it forms an umbrella for those aspects of contemporary practice that defy the rigid traditional categories. I'm interested in a tradition of change rather than stasis. It has always seemed natural to me to want to involve the whole self-body literally and metaphorically in the work.

What connects me to other artists, in whatever medium, are ideas – a commonality based upon ways of seeing, of being in the world. My relationship to an audience changes from piece to piece but I usually think in terms of the quality of relationship of the work to one other person rather than a group. I'm not interested in spectacle. I've worked outdoors in cities on a number of occasions. Street work was necessary in order to explore all possible meanings of a particular image-idea. Live art now has a system of funding and promotion – great. But much of the work is theatre. Yes, there is a difference, which would not be a problem except that the theatrical-based work tends to undermine the philosophical basis of visual arts ideas. It's important that roots are not cut off.

Photo: Kathy Schick. 'Live Head Legacy' was a five-hour performance-action at the New Gallery, Calgary, Canada, 1989.

20 • Contacts

Live art promoters

The following list has been compiled in association with the Regional Arts Boards for the benefit of artists working in live art and who are seeking bookings for their work. It is intended as a guide only, and should not be taken as an 'approved' or comprehensive list of promoters.

Arnolfini, 16 Narrow Quay, Prince Street, Bristol BS1 4AQ. Tel 0272 299191. Diane Warden (Programmer)

Artangel Trust, 133 Oxford Street, London W1R 1TD. Tel 071 434 2887. Michael Morris/James Lingwood

ArtsAdmin, 295 Kentish Town Road, London NW5 2TJ. Tel 071 482 3631/3753. Judith Knight

Bluecoat Arts Centre, School Lane, Liverpool L1 3BX. Tel 051 708 8877.

Brighton Festival, Marlborough House, 54 Old Steine, Brighton BN1 1EQ. Tel 0273 298 01. Gavin Henderson

Cartwright Hall, Lister Park, Bradford BD9 4NS. Tel 0274 493313. Caroline Krzesinska

Castle Museum, Nottingham NG1 6EL. Tel 0602 483504. Jane Bevan

Chapter Arts Centre, Market Road, Cardiff CF5 1QE. Tel 0222 396 061. Janet Alexander

Chisenhale Dance Space, 64-84 Chisenhale Road, London E3 5QZ. Tel 081 981 6617. Amanda Leon

Chisenhale Gallery/Studios, 64-84 Chisenhale Road, London E3 5QZ. Tel 081 981 4518. Jonathan Watkins

City of Nottingham Arts Department, 51 Castle Gate, Nottingham NG1 6AF. Tel 0602 483504. David Metcalfe

Cleveland Gallery, Victoria Road, Middlesborough TS1 3QS. Tel 0642 225408. Jane Warillow

Dean Clough Gallery, Industrial Park, Halifax HX3 5AX. Tel 0422 344555. Mary Sarah

Edge Biennale Trust, PO Box 744, London N1. Tel 071 729 3007. Rob La Frenais/Jon Bewley

Edinburgh Festival Society, 21 Market Street, Edinburgh EH1 1BW. Tel 031 226 4001. Bryan McMaster

Eventspace, 12a Bellhaven Terrace Glasgow G12 041 357 4924

Ferens Art Gallery, Queen Victoria Square, Hull HU1 3RA. Tel 0482 593912. Louise Karlsen

Film and Video Umbrella, Top Floor, Chelsea Reach, 79-89 Lots Road, London SW10 0RN. Tel 071 376 3171. Emily Grant, Steven Bird & Moira Sweeney

The Green Room, 54-56 Whitworth Street West, Manchester M1 5WW. Tel 061 236 1676. Lawrence Lane

Harris Museum and Art Gallery, Market Square, Preston PR1 2PP. Tel 0772 58248. James Green

Hull Time Based Arts, 8 Posterngate, Hull HU1 2JN. Tel 0482 216446. Mike Stubbs

ICA, 12 Carlton House Terrace, London SW1Y 5AH. Tel 071 930 0493. Mik Flood (Director), Iwona Blaswick/Emma Dexter (Exhibitions)

Ikon Gallery, 58 - 72 John Bright Street, Brimingham B1 1BN. Tel 021 643 0708. Angela Kingston

Kettles Yard, Castle Street, Cambridge CB3 0AQ. Tel 0223 352124. Anna Harding/Charles Escher

Laing Art Gallery, Higham Place, Newcastle-upon-Tyne NE1 8AG. Tel 091 232 7734. Mike Collier

Liverpool Festival of Comedy, Bluecoat Chambers , School Lane, Liverpool L1 3BX. 051 709 815. Jayne Casey

London Mime Festival, Hetherington Seelig, 35 Little Russell Street, London WC1A 2HH. Tel 071 637 5661. Joseph Seelig

London Video Access, 5-7 Buck Street, Camden, London, NW1 8NJ. Michael Maziere

Manchester City Art Gallery, Moseley Street/ Princess Street, Manchester, M2 3JL. Tel 061 236 5244. Tim Wilcox

Mayfest,18 Albion Street, Glasgow G1 1LH. Tel 041 552 8000. Robert Robson

Museum of Installation, 33 Great Sutton Street, London EC1 V0DX. Tel 071 582 1588

Museum of Modern Art, 30 Pembroke Street, Oxford OX1 1BP. Tel 0865 722733. John Leslie

Paley Wright (formerly Interim Art), 20 Dering Street, London W1R 9AA. Tel 071 495 4580. Maureen Pale & Glenn Scott Wright

Phoenix Arts Centre, 11 Newarke Street, Leicester LE1 5SS. Tel 0533 554854. Nigel Hinds

Prema, South Street, Uley, Dursley. GL11 5SS. Tel 0453 860703

Projects UK, Black Swan Court, Westgate Road, Newcastle-upon-Tyne NE1 1SG. Tel 091 261 4527. Simon Herbert

Quarter Club, Green Room, 54-56 Whitworth Street West, Manchester M1 5WW. Tel 061 236 1676

Riverside Studios, Crisp Road, London W6 9RL. Tel. 081 741 2251/081 748 3354 box office. Jonathan Lamede Director/Zoe Sherman (Exhibitions)

Rochdale Art Gallery, Esplanade, Rochdale OL16 1AQ. Tel 0706 342154. Jill Morgan

Serpentine Gallery, Kensington Gardens, London W2 3XA. Tel 071 402 6075

Southampton Art Gallery, Civic Centre, Southampton, SO9 4XF. Tel 0703 223855 ext 769

Stoke on Trent City Museum & Art Gallery, Bethesda Street, Hanley, Stoke on Trent. Tel 0782 202173. Jennifer Rennie

The Tate Gallery, Millbank, London SW1P 4RG. Tel 071 821 1313. Richard Humphries

Third Eye Centre, 350 Sauchiehall Street, Glasgow G2 3J D. Tel 041 332 7521 (at the time of going to press Third Eye was being wound up due to insolvency)

Transmission Gallery, 28 King Street, Trongate, Glasgow G15 HQP. Tel 041 552 4813. Christine Borlands

TSWA c/o Jonathen Harvey, 15 Robinson Road, Bethnal Green, London E2 9LX.

Tyne International, 6 Higham Place, Newcastle-upon-Tyne NE1 8AF. Tel 091 230 4394. James Peto

Watermans Art Centre, 40 High Street, Brentford TW8 0DS. Tel 081 847 5651. Rachel Clare (Theatre)

Wolverhampton Art Gallery, Lichfield Street, Wolverhampton WV1 1DU. Tel 0902 312032. Krysia Rozanska

The Zap Club, 17 Tichbourne Street, Brighton BN1 1UR. Tel 0273 821588. Neil Butler

Live art funding bodies

The Arts Council, 14 Great Peter Street, London SW1P 3NQ. Tel 071 333 0100. Performance Art Officer; Art Officer; Film and Video Officer; Drama Officer

The Scottish Arts Council, 12 Manor Place, Edinburgh EH3 7DD. Tel 031 226 6051. Art Officer

Welsh Arts Council, Holst House, 9 Museum Place, Cardiff CF1 3NX. Tel 0222 394711. Director of Art,

Arts Council of Northern Ireland, 181a Stranmillis Road, Belfast BT9 5DU. Tel 0232 381 591. Visual arts department

Regional arts boards (replacing regional arts associations)

Eastern Arts Board, Assistant Visual Arts Officer, Cherry Hinton Hall, Cherry Hinton Road, Cambridge CB1 4DW. Tel 0223 215355. (covers Bedfordshire, Cambridge, Essex, Hertfordshire, Lincolnshire, Norfolk, Sussex)

East Midlands Arts Board, Visual Arts Officer, Mountfields House, Forest Road, Loughborough LE11 3HU. Tel 0509 218292. (covers Leicestershire, Nottinghamshire, Northamptonshire and part of Derbyshire, not the High Peak District)

London Arts Board, Visual Arts Officer, Coriander Building, 20 Gainsford Street, London, SE1 2NE. Tel 071 403 9013. (covers Greater London area)

Northern Arts Board, Visual Arts Officer, 10 Osborne Terrace, Newcastle-upon-Tyne NE2 1NZ. Tel 091 281 6334. (covers Cleveland, Cumbria, Durham, Northumberland, Tyne & Wear)

Arts Board North West, Visual Arts Officer, 4th Floor, 12 Harter Street, Manchester M1 6HY. Tel 061 228 3062. (covers Cheshire, Greater Manchester, Lancashire, Merseyside, and the High Peak area of Derbyshire)

Southern Arts Board, Visual Arts Officer, 13 St Clements Street, Winchester SO23 9UQ. Tel 0962 55099. (covers Berkshire, Buckinghamshire, Hampshire, Isle of Wight, Oxfordshire, Wiltshire and the Poole, Bournemouth and Christchurch areas of Dorset)

South East Arts Board, Drama Officer, 10 Mount Ephraim, Tunbridge Wells TN4 8AS. Tel 0892 515210. (covers Kent, Surrey and Sussex, excluding Greater London Areas)

South West Arts Board, Visual Arts Officer, Bradninch Place, Gandy Street, Exeter EX4 3LS. Tel 0392 218188. (covers Avon, Cornwall, Devon and Dorset, except Bournemouth, Christchurch and Poole, Gloucestershire and Somerset)

West Midlands Arts Board, Visual Arts Officer, 82 Granville Street, Birmingham B1 2LH. Tel 021 631 3121. (covers Hereford &Worcester, Shropshire, Staffordshire, Warwickshire & West Midlands)

Yorkshire and Humberside Arts Board, Visual Arts Officer, Glyde House, Glydegate, Bradford BD5 OBQ. Tel 0274 723051. (covers Humberside and North, South and West Yorkshire)

Other sources

Department of Visual Arts, The British Council, 10 Spring Gardens, London SW1 82BN. Tel 071 930 8466

Arts Project Unit, The British Council, 10 Spring Gardens, London SW1 82BN. Tel 071 930 8466

Calouste Gulbenkian Foundation, 98 Portland Place, London WIN 4ET. Tel 071 636 5313

Public Art Forum, c/o City Gallery Arts Trust, Great Barn, Great Linford, Milton Keynes MK14 5DZ. Tel 0908 606 791

Polytechnics & colleges supporting live art

Brighton Polytechnic, Faculty of Art, Design and Humanities, Grand Parade, Brighton, East Sussex BN2 2JY. Tel 0273 600900

Cardiff Institute of Higher Education, Faculty of Art and Design, Howard Gardens, Cardiff CF2 1SP. Tel 0222 55111. Anthony Howell

Central St Martins College of Art and Design, Southampton Row, London WC1B 4AP. Tel 071 753 9090. Monica Ross

Dartington College of Arts, Dartington Hall, Totnes, Devon TO9 6EJ. Tel 0803 862224. Rose Garrard

Humberside Polytechnic, School of Art, Architecture and Design, Kingston-upon-Hull, North Humberside HU1 3DG. Tel 0482 440550. Willis Aynley

Leicester Polytechnic, Leicester School of Arts, PO Box 143, Leicester LE1 9BH. Tel 0533 551551

Newcastle upon Tyne Polytechnic, Faculty of Art and Design, Squires Building, Sandyford Road, Newcastle-upon-Tyne NE1 8ST. Tel 092 232 6002. Chris Wainwright

Nottingham Polytechnic, Faculty of Art and Design, Burton Street, Nottingham NG1 4BU. Tel 0602 418418. Robert Ayres

Sheffield Polytechnic, School of Cultural Studies, Psalter Lane, Sheffield S11 8UZ. Tel 0742 720911. Fran Hegarty

Slade School of Art, University College, Gower Street, London WC1. Tel 071 387 7050. Stuart Brisley

University of Ulster, Faculty of Art and Design, York Street, Belfast, BT15 1ED. Tel 0232 328515. Alastair Maclennan

Wimbledon School of Art, Merton Hall Road, London, SW19 3QA. Tel 081 540 0231. Richard Layzell

Wolverhampton Polytechnic, School of Art and Design, Molineux Street, Wolverhampton, WV1 1SB. Tel 0902 321963

Other training organisations

Welfare State International, The Ellers, Ulverston, Cumbria, LA12 OAA. Tel 0229 581127. Sue Gill

21 • Further reading

Body, Space, Image: Notes towards improvisation and performance. Miranda Tufnell and Chris Crickmay, Virago, 1990, £12.99, ISBN 1 853811 31 9. Available from Grantham Book Services, Issac Newton Way, Alma Park Industrial Estate, NG31 9SD.) Improvisation for individuals and groups and its interaction with the space and the performance itself.

Class Myths & Culture. Stefan Szczelkun, Working Press, 1990, £5.95, ISBN 1 870736 03 6. (Available from 85 St. Agnes Place, Kennington, London, SE11 4BB.) A collection of essays which address the issues of class and culture, with reports on three large scale collaborative performance art events which relate to urban communities.

Cultural Grounding: Live Art & Cultural Diversity (Discussion Paper). Michael McMillan, Arts Council, 1990. (Available from Live Art Unit, Arts Council of Great Britain, 14 Great Peter Street, London, SW1P 3NQ.)

Doing it right in LA: Self producing for the performing artist. Jacki Apple, AA Astro Artz and Fringe, 1990, $12.00, ISBN 0 937122 13 0. (Available from Fringe Festival Los Angeles, 6380 Wilshire Blvd., Suite 147, Los Angeles, CA 90048, USA.) A resource book for performing artists which covers everything from choosing the site, making a budget, selecting performers, finding materials, publicity and promotion and the performance itself.

Engineers of the Imagination. Tony Coult & Baz Kershaw (Eds), Welfare State International, 2nd ed 1990, £ 8.95, ISBN 0 413 52800 6. (Available from AN Publications, PO Box 23, Sunderland, SR4 6DG. Tel 091 514 3600.) A practical guide to creating processions, large scale puppets and sculptures, fixed structures, fire and ice technology, shadow puppets, processional theatre and dance music and celebratory food and feasts. Includes examples of previous Welfare State International Projects.

Live Art Now. Gray Watson & Jeni Walwin, Arts Council of Great Britain, 1987. (Available from Arts Council of Great Britain, 14 Great Peter Street, London, SW1P 3NQ.) A review of performance art funded by the Arts Council in the 1980's and an examination of the historical contexts in which it has developed.

Peformance Art: From Futurism to the Present. Rosalee Goldberg, Thames and Hudson, 2nd ed 1988, £4.95, ISBN 0 500 20214 1. (Available from 30 Bloomsbury Street, London, WC1B 3QP.) A revised edition which examines important developments in performance art up to 1986.

Performance Art Memoirs: Volume 1. Jeff Nuttall, John Calder, 1979, £4.95 ISBN 0 7145 3788 X. (Available from 9/15 Neal Street, London, WC2H 9TV)

Performance Art Memoirs: Volume 2 scripts. Jeff Nuttall, John Calder, 1979, £4.95 ISBN 0 7145 378 96. (Available from 9/15 Neal Street, London, WC2H 9TV)

Specialist performance magazines

High Performance (Available from 1641 18th Street, Santa Monica, CA 90404, USA - annual UK subscription $28 surface, $55 airmail.). A quarterly magazine published in the US *'devoted to progressive thinking in the arts'*. Includes features and reviews.

Live Art Listings (Available from Live Art Listings, Visual Arts Department, Arts Council of Great Britain, 14 Great Peter Street, London, SW1P 3NQ.) A new free bi-monthly listing service to be launched in January 1992 which will cover live and time-based art, radical theatre and movement work, mixed media projects and news.

Peformance (Available from PO Box 717, London, SW5 9BS – annual UK individual subscription £18.00.) Published quarterly, 'Performance' covers all avant garde art, particularly that which crosses the boundaries of traditional art disciplines.

Art magazines which cover live art

Artists Newsletter (Available from AN Publications, PO Box 23, Sunderland, SR4 6DG - annual individual subscription £15). A monthly magazine relevant to all practice in the visual arts with "live art" and "film & Video" opportunities columns, listings of live art events in the exhibitions section and articles.

Art Rage (Available from 28 Skaklewell Lane, London, E8 2A2, tel 071 254 7275 – annual subscription £10). Covers all the arts across the spectrum of Black cultures.

Feminist Art News (Available from Unit 26, 30-38 Dock Street, Leeds, LS10 1JF – annual subscription £9). Published quarterly, FAN looks at feminist issues across all artforms.

Independent Media (Available from 7, Campbell Court, Bramley, Basingstoke, Hampshire, RG26 5EG - Annual subscription £15 for individuals). A film, video and television monthly with news, information, listings and articles.

Variant (Available from 2/9 73 Robertson Street, Glasgow, G2 8QD - annual subscription £12). A quarterly magazine which aims to cross the boundaries of art, cultural and critical activity.

Womens Art Magazine (Available from The Womens Artists Slide Library, Fulham Palace, Bishops Avenue, London, SW6 6EA - annual subscription £15). A bi-monthly magazine covering all visual art practices.

Books from AN Publications

AN Publications specialises in publishing and distributing practical information and advice for all working in the visual arts. Listed below are a selection of books which will be helpful for people working in live and performance art. All prices are inclusive of postage and books are available by mail order from AN Publications, FREEPOST, PO Box 23, Sunderland, SR1 1BR or by credit card on 091 514 3600. For a comprehensive listing of all our titles please see the order form at the end of this book.

Artists Handbooks 3: Money Matters. Sarah Deeks, Richard Murphy & Sally Nolan, AN Publications, 1991, £7.25, ISBN 0 907730 11 6. Reliable, friendly advice on keeping accounts, employing people and everything to do with finances.

Artists Handbooks 4: Copyright. Roland Miller, AN Publications, 1991, £7.25, ISBN 0 907730 12 4. Essentail advice on negotiating copyright agreements and dealing with the infringement of copyright.

Artists Handbooks 5: Organising your exhibition. Debbie Duffin, AN Publications, 1991, £7.25, ISBN 0 907730 14 0. A practical guide offering advice on finding space, finances, publicity, insurance, framing and hanging work, private views and selling.

Directory of Exhibition Spaces. Susan Jones, AN Publications, 2nd ed, 1989, £12.50, ISBN 0 907730 05 1. A comprehensive lisiting of over 2000 galleries in the UK and Eire with details of type of work shown and how to apply.

Making Ways. David Bulter (ed), AN Publications, 2nd ed, 1989, £11.99, ISBN 0 907730 078. First hand advice from artists and craftspeople on everything your need to know as a professional artist. Topics covered include exhibiting, public art, using skills, promotion, studios, financial support, business, safety, training, funding, etc with an extensive list of contacts.

Arts Funding Guide. Anne-Maire Doulton, Directory of Social Change, 2nd ed, 1991, £14.00, ISBN 0 907164 72 2. A guide to fund-raising for arts organisations.

The Handbook of Grants. Graeme Farnell, Museum Development Company, 1990, £15.95, ISBN 1 873114 00 1. A listing of all grants available from public sources for visual arts organisations.

Factpack 1: Rates of Pay '91. Susan Jones, AN Publications, 1991, £1.50. Updated information on rates of pay for artists with guidelines on establishing an hourly rate.

Factpack 3: Mailing the press. David Butler & Caroline Lambert, AN Publications, 1991, £1.50. Guidelines on writing a press release plus a listing of UK art press.

Factpack 4: Getting TV & Radio Coverage. Paul Gough & Caroline Lambert, AN Publications, 1991, £1.50. Includes a contact list of TV and radio stations.

22 • Index

Other AN Publications

AN Publications is the only publisher to specialise in information for visual artists, photographers, time-based artists and craftspeople. So if you need to know:

what awards, competitions and opportunities are in the offing
which galleries are worth approaching to show your work
how to make the most of your skills
who supplies 'green' art materials
where to find help, information and advice
when to apply for grants

and any other practical information, we can help you through our directories, handbooks, 'Fact Packs' and monthly magazine, *Artists Newsletter.*

Artists Newsletter The essential monthly magazine packed with up-to-the-minute information on residencies, awards, commissions, jobs, competitions, etc. The visual artist's 'lifeline'.

Making Ways ***The visual artist's guide to surviving and thriving.*** Written by artists for artists, with first-hand advice on all aspects 'business' practice. 368 pages.

Directory of Exhibition Spaces A comprehensive listing of over 2000 exhibition spaces in the UK and Eire to help you find the ideal space for your work. 500 pages.

Residencies in Education: ***setting them up and making them work.*** Explores the strengths and weaknesses of 6 residencies, to help you get the best out of placements of all kinds.124 pages.

Health & Safety: ***making art & avoiding dangers.*** Advice on health and safety across all art and craft forms. Plus help on preparing COSHH assessments. 128 pages.

Money Matters: ***the artist's financial guide.*** User-friendly advice on: tax, national insurance, keeping accounts, pricing work and much more. Features an accounting system devised for artists. 128 pages.

Copyright: ***protection, use & responsibilities.*** Essential advice on negotiating copyright agreements, exploiting earning and promotional potential, and dealing with infringments. 128 pages.

Organising your Exhibition: ***the self help guide.*** Excellent advice on all aspects of organising exhibitions, from dealing with printers to buying wine. 128 pages.

Across Europe:	***the artist's personal guide to opportunity and action.*** Artist's first hand experiences in 20 European nations help you take your first steps into europe. 200 pages.
Independent Photography Directory	Listing of over 250 organisations involved with photography plus awards, fellowships, funding bodies, press lists, etc. 224 pages.
Code of Practice for Independent Photography	Guidelines for successful negotiations with advice on employment, copyright, exhibiting, commissions... plus sample fees and rates of pay. 32 pages.
FACT PACKS	Indispensible factsheets for artists, makers and administrators.
Rates of Pay	Information on current pay rates for artists.
Slide Indexes	Includes a national listing of artists' registers and slide indexes.
Mailing the Press	Includes a press list of national dailies, weeklies, and magazines.
Getting TV & Radio Coverage	Includes a contact list of TV and radio stations.
Craft Fairs	Includes a selected list of national and international fairs with details.
Insurance	Advises on types of insurance artists need, and why.
Post-graduate courses	A detailed listing of post-graduate courses in the UK.
Green Art Materials	A listing of 'green' art products and suppliers.
New Technology for Artists	Includes a listing of supplier's, courses and hands-on facilities.
Basic Survival Facts	Essential practical information for all new artist's on getting started.
OTHER BOOKS	We also supply books produced by other publishers covering areas such as fundraising, crafts and illustration. Please ask for our brochure.

ORDER FORM

Only UK prices given, phone for overseas prices		Qty	£
A Code of Practice for Photography	£3.25		
Across Europe	£9.95		
Copyright	£7.25		
Directory of Exhibition Spaces	£12.50		
Health & Safety	£7.25		
Independent Photography Directory	£5.00		
Organising Your Exibition	£7.25		
Making Ways	£11.99		
Money Matters	£7.25		
Residencies in Education	£7.25		
Artists Newsletter **£15.00 UK individual, £25.00 UK institution** Annual subscription beginning with ______	issue		
Fact Pack 1: Rates of Pay	£1.50		
Fact Pack 2: Slide Indexes	£1.50		
Fact Pack 3: Mailing the Press	£1.50		
Fact Pack 4: Getting TV & Radio Coverage	£1.50		
Fact Pack 5 : Craft Fairs	£1.50		
Fact Pack 6: Insurance	£1.50		
Fact Pack 7: Post-graduate Courses	£1.50		
Fact Pack 8: Green Art Materials	£1.50		
Fact Pack 9: New Technology	£1.50		
Basic Survival Facts	£1.50		
		TOTAL	

Name/Address

Name

Address

Postcode Telephone

Payment by cheque/postal order

Send cheque/postal order made payable to AN Publications

Return to: AN Publications, FREEPOST, PO Box 23, Sunderland SR1 1BR

Payment by credit card NB Visa/MasterCard only

Card number

Expiry date

Return to: AN Publications, FREEPOST, PO Box 23, Sunderland SR1 1BR

Credit card telephone orders 091 514 3600 (Mon – Fri 9-5)

❑ Please send me a free sample issue of Artists Newsletter

AN Publications also distributes books for the visual arts produced by other publishers, ask for our full publication list.

If you found this book useful...

...help us stay in touch with your needs and interests by filling in and returning this freepost form. Your opinions are important, and will help us to continue to publish the kinds of books you need, when you need them. To thank you for your help, we will send you a discount voucher for use when purchasing other books from AN Publications.

Title of book ______________________________

Where did you buy it? ______________________________

Why did you choose it?

- ❐ Best coverage of the subject
- ❐ Recognised the author
- ❐ Recognised the publisher
- ❐ The price was right
- ❐ Other (please specify) ______________________________

Where did you hear about this book?

- ❐ Book review in ______________________________
- ❐ Leaflet in ______________________________
- ❐ Advertisement in ______________________________
- ❐ Browsing in ______________________________ bookshop
- ❐ Personal recommendation
- ❐ Other (please specify) ______________________________

Have you any comments on the content of this book?

____

____

____

____

____

Thank you for taking the time to fill in this form. Where shall we send your discount voucher?

Name ______________________________

Address ______________________________

______________________________ **Postcode** ______________________________

SEND TO: **Lynn Evans**
AN Publications, Freepost, PO Box 23, Sunderland SR1 1BR